AC COBRA

Other Titles In The Crowood AutoClassics Series

Ferrari Dino	Anthony Curtis
Jaguar E-Type	Jonathan Wood
Lamborghini Countach	Peter Dron
Lotus Elan	Mike Taylor
MGB	Brian Laban
Porsche 911	David Vivian
Triumph TRs	Graham Robson
Sprites and Midgets	Anders Ditlev Clausager
Lotus Esprit	Jeremy Walton
Jensen Interceptor	John Tipler

AC COBRA

The Complete Story

Brian Laban

CROWOOD AUTOCLASSICS

First published in 1991 by
The Crowood Press Ltd
Gipsy Lane, Swindon
Wiltshire, SN2 6DQ

British Library Cataloguing in Publication Data

Laban, Brian
    AC Cobra.
    1. AC Cobra racing sports cars
    I. Title
    629.228

    ISBN 1 85223 459 8

Acknowledgements

The photographs and line-drawings in this book were kindly
supplied by The Motoring Picture Library, Beaulieu, AC Cars Ltd;
the Ford Motor Company Ltd Photographic Services and *Autocar
and Motor*.

Typeset by Taurus Graphics, Abingdon, Oxon.
Printed in England by Richard Clay Ltd

Contents

Cobra – a Brief History   6
Introduction   9
1   Carroll Shelby BC (Before the Cobra)   14
2   AC – The Company   26
3   The Ace   46
4   Developing the Cobra   66
5   Into Production: the Leaf-Spring Cars   83
6   Coil Springs and the Mighty 427   107
7   The Competition Roadsters   135
8   The Daytona Coupe   157
9   The More Distant Relatives   173
10   Driving and Ownership   187
11   Dodge Viper and Shelby after the Cobra   196
Appendix   203
Index   205

COBRA – A BRIEF HISTORY

October 1953	AC Ace, based on Tojeiro twin-tube chassis and with AC engine, unveiled at Earls Court Motor Show, London.
1956	Ace available with Bristol six-cylinder engine.
1958	Ford lightweight small-block V8 engine programme started in USA.
December 1960	Carroll Shelby races for the last time, at Riverside; plans to build sports car.
March 1961	British Ford six-cylinder engine tried in Ace as supplies of Bristol engine threatened by Bristol switching to Chrysler V8 power.
September 1961	Shelby contacts AC with ideas for V8-engined sports car based on AC Ace.
November 1961	First 'lightweight' Ford V8 engines delivered to AC via Shelby.
Winter 1961–62	AC and Shelby working on first Cobra prototype in Thames Ditton.
January 1962	Prototype Cobra runs for the first time, at Silverstone, probably with 221cu in engine.
February 1962	Engine removed and first prototype, chassis no. CSX2000, shipped to Shelby in Santa Fe Springs. Car quickly fitted with 260 engine and tested at Riverside.
April 1962	Cobra introduced to press and first shown in public at New York Auto Show.
May 1962	First magazine tests of prototype Cobra appear.
July 1962	First three 'production' Cobras completed and shipped to USA; further cars followed soon after, all using 260 V8.
October 1962	First Cobra raced for first time, by Billy Krause at Riverside before he retired.
January 1963	First 289 Cobra completed, chassis no. CSX2075.
January 1963	Cobra's first race win, at Riverside.
March 1963	First production rack-and-pinion Cobra completed, chassis no. CSX2127.
June 1963	Two Cobras entered at Le Mans: one retired; the other finished seventh overall.
Late 1963	AC Ace ceases production.
October 1963	First 427-engined prototype built using leaf-spring chassis.
November 1963	First right-hand-drive Cobra delivered in UK.
November 1963	Work started on racing coupe project which would become Daytona.

February 1964	First Daytona coupe, based on chassis no. CSX2287, tested at Riverside. Took three GT class wins during 1964, and fourth overall at Le Mans.
March 1964	Ken Miles raced prototype 427, on leaf-spring chassis no. CSX2166, at Sebring; crashed in practice, and was retired from race.
April 1964	AC tested own 289 coupe at Le Mans, on leaf-spring chassis no. 'A98'.
November 1964	Leaf-spring chassis production for export stopped.
December 1964	Second 427 prototype 'Flip-Top', on chassis no. CSX2196, débuted by Miles at Nassau Speed Weeks.
January 1965	Production 427 announced, with totally redesigned coil-spring chassis and heavily revised body. Coil-spring chassis nos. start at CSX3001.
March 1965	Leaf-spring chassis production ended completely after 655 cars built.
Early 1965	Work in hand on 427 'Super Coupe' in USA and UK, but project eventually abandoned (car, on chassis no. CSX3054) finally completed by private owner, 1980.
1965	Daytona won World Manufacturers' Championship for GT cars, with six GT class wins.
October 1965	AC showed Frua-bodied AC 428 at Earls Court.
May 1966	AC start producing 289-engined version of coil-spring chassis for European market.
February 1968	Five special long-wheelbase chassis built for Paramount Pictures film.
February 1969	Final coil-spring car completed, in European series, after a total of 348 built.
1969	Eight 427-type coil-spring-type chassis built by AC for US-based electric car project, on chassis nos. EFX501–508; several later converted to 427 replicas.
1980	Autokraft Mk4 introduced, based on original coil-spring Cobra chassis and body tooling.
February 1982	Autokraft granted rights to use AC logo on Mk4; soon after, Brian Angliss bought controlling interest in AC Cars Ltd.
October 1987	Ford buy controlling interest in AC from Angliss.
Mid-1990	Ford announce intentions to wind up AC Cars Ltd, but Angliss fights decision and continues building AC Mk4 Cobra, now including limited edition lightweight version.

Introduction

If you are ever struggling to think of the precise definition of the words 'sports car', do not look in a dictionary, go and look at a Shelby AC Cobra. *That* is a sports car.

The Cobra was a fairy tale, a car created out of the simplest of ingredients along the age-old lines of competent but uncomplicated European chassis and big but un- sophisticated US engine. That really was about all there was to it, but the Cobra was one of those rare cars that is much more than the sum of its parts.

As a road-car, it redefined the limits of straightline performance. As a racer, it started by cleaning up against the Corvettes and Jaguars in American club racing, and it

The 'small' Cobra, the classic 289, retained most of the delicacy of the Ace even in later and rather more rounded AC 289 form – combining the small-block engine with the coil-spring chassis of the 427, for European consumption only.

just steadily grew in stature. Eventually, it beat Ferrari in the World Sports Car Manufacturers' Championship.

The Cobra was a great car, but it was not unique nor even particularly innovative. It used basic engineering well, but really nothing more. It was only styled in so far as the 1950s shape that it was based on had to be fleshed out to accommodate the added muscle. It had the might of Ford, one of the world's Big Three motor manufacturers, behind it, but it was hardly pushed commercially; and it only lasted seven years in all (if you do not count the current AC MkIV) from the first production 260 to the final European spec AC 289.

For all the legend, the Cobra was strictly a limited edition success. If every original Cobra owner in the world bought a copy of this book we would be talking 1030 sales, that is 655 leaf-spring cars, including the original 260s and the first series of 289s, 348 coil-spring 427s (including the majority that were really 428s), and 27 coil-sprung, 289-engined AC MkIIIs, for Europe only. We could add a few AC MkIV owners, but not many.

But if everyone who ever *wanted* a Cobra bought the book, it would be high in the bestseller lists for years to come. The Cobra is that kind of car.

THE MAGIC INGREDIENT

The magic extra ingredient that made the Cobra work where so many similar concepts before and after it failed, was one Carroll Shelby, son of a Texas mailman, sometime military flying instructor, haulage contractor, oil-field wrangler and failed chicken farmer, former racing driver, Le Mans winner, all-round good guy.

Beating Ferrari in a World Championship was sweet for Shelby. Like many others he had crossed the iconoclastic *Ingegnere* on a bad day, felt his withering sarcasm for lesser

Father of the Cobra, Carroll Shelby – the man in the right place at the right time with the right vision to bring American and European thinking together.

mortals and told him on the spot that one day he would come back and 'beat his ass'. A lot of people said that to Ferrari over the years. Ferruccio Lamborghini did it with several of his road cars but never threw down the racing gauntlet; Shelby hit Ferrari where it really hurt, on the racetrack.

What must have riled Ferrari even more was that the laconic Texan did it relatively simply, without great engineering sophistication, and backed by Ford money at a time in the 1960s when Ferrari was just declining to be bought out lock, stock, and barrel by the Dearborn giant.

Shelby, of course, was not the first would-be sports car builder to put a big American lump into a small European chassis. He was not even the first to put a US V8 into an AC Ace. Briggs Cunningham had squeezed a 5.5-litre Cadillac engine into the first Healey Silverstone to reach the USA, which was a bit more radical than the standard Riley engine. That was the seed of all the later Cunninghams, especially the ones that went racing at Le Mans and showed that US racers could go round right-hand corners too. British driver Tommy Cole, tragically killed at Le Mans in 1953, is credited with starting a trend in the early 1950s by being the first to shoehorn a Cadillac V8 into a very British Allard chassis, creating a beast with a 150mph (241kph) top speed and under 6-second 0–60mph (96.5kph) capabilities. Shelby himself carved quite an amateur and semi-professional racing career with various US V8-engined Allards – one of the few cars reckoned to be even more fearsome than the mighty 427 Cobra later turned out to be.

Several other manufacturers could have taken up Shelby's vision and produced the Cobra: he hawked his scheme to General Motors, Aston Martin, Jensen, and Healey among others before AC took him up on the idea, and even AC may have bought it more out of desperation than out of vision.

TOTAL PERFORMANCE

To understand the Cobra, you really have to understand Carroll Shelby, and especially the way Carroll Shelby was in 1961, when he had been forced to give up motor racing and desperately needed a new challenge. You also need to understand why Ford had suddenly changed from a worthy but dull image in the Ford Safety Campaign to the other extreme and what they came to call Total Performance. Understanding all this means knowing a little bit about Lee Iacocca, who is now boss of Chrysler and staunch supporter of what many people see as the Cobra for the 1990s – the Dodge Viper. Shelby has a hand in that too, of course.

There are lots of other personalities in the Cobra story: the Hurlock brothers who controlled AC and had the imagination to take on Shelby's ideas; John Tojeiro who effectively fathered the Ace, without which there would have been no Cobra; Peter Brock and especially Ken Miles who took the Cobra by the scruff of the neck and tested and tuned it until it worked; Phil Remington who Shelby respected as both a great engineer and a great administrator; Dave Evans of Ford who gave Shelby the engine he needed; and everyone else who simply believed in miracles.

After Shelby and AC, the Cobra story has to start with the Ace, the pretty and fine-handling sports car that dragged AC's image out of the doldrums and turned it back into a sporting marque. After the demise of the superb but outdated six-cylinder Bristol, the Ace was a car looking for an engine at exactly the same time as Shelby was a man looking for a car.

The Cobra first emerged early in 1962, with a 260cu in (4,261cc) V8. Before the end of 1962, it had gained the 289cu in (4,736cc) development of the 260 and had had its baptism in racing. By 1963 it had appeared at Le Mans and was becoming a prolific winner in lesser events.

In 1964, the strictly limited edition coupe made its debut at Daytona, which gave it a convenient name, and in the same year Shelby contrived the fearsome 427 around Ford's monstrously powerful NASCAR stock-racing engine. The 427 demanded a substantially revised chassis, bigger and stronger but also with coil spring suspension in place of the old transverse leaves. That also meant a more aggressively bulbous body, and by 1965 the 427 was in production – mainly to gain homologation for racing.

Many of the '427s' for the road were actually fitted with the Ford 428 'police-spec' Galaxie engine, a powerful option in itself, but nothing like so rabid as the race-bred 427. In Europe, AC continued to put 289 engines into the new 427 chassis as the AC 289, which was perhaps the most refined Cobra of them all, but only built in tiny numbers.

BEATING FERRARI

In 1965, Shelby finally did beat Ferrari, taking the World Manufacturers' Championship for GT Cars with the 289-engined Daytona coupes – and then withdrawing the Daytonas from international racing.

Time was running out for the Cobra, not because of any shortcomings with the car beyond those that it had always had, but because attitudes to the automobile were changing in the USA (and eventually around the world), and because increasingly restrictive environmentally protective legislation was closing in. It was the end of the muscle car era in America, and effectively the end of the Cobra as a production car. The 427 went out of production during 1967, and AC's European-spec 289 lasted until 1969, but with less than 30 cars built.

The Cobra was one of the last of the great no-holds-barred sports cars. After the Cobra,

Beauty and the beast: the light and lithe-looking early 289 road car is dwarfed by the full-race 427 in Shelby colours.

Coping with 427 power obliged the Cobra to grow markedly bigger, mainly to accommodate enough rubber to put the massive torque of Ford's NASCAR-bred engine on to the road.

raw power increasingly gave way to sophistication; supercars came to be something else entirely – quick but rarely so devastatingly quick as any of the Cobras, and hardly ever with an open top.

That people still rank the Cobra among the all-time greats is evident in the enormous prices paid for the genuine article (especially any car with a racing history), in the success of the current AC MkIV (which is a genuine Cobra in everything but date), and even in the extraordinary market for Cobra replicas (varying in quality from the sublime to the ridiculous).

It is an extraordinary success story based on not much more than a simple tubular chassis and a basically unremarkable cast-iron production engine.

1 Carroll Shelby BC (Before the Cobra)

Carroll Hall Shelby is a remarkable man. In the early 1960s, all the basic ingredients for the Cobra already existed. The AC Ace had been around in various guises since 1953 and, in spite of struggling slightly since the demise of the superb Bristol six-cylinder engine in 1961, it was not quite ready for the scrapheap yet. Ford's new generation lightweight cast-iron small-block V8 engine had just been developed for the mid-size Fairlane, via a Canadian truck engine.

Even the philosophy that could have brought the two elements together was by no means out of the ordinary. Any number of would-be sports car manufacturers had shoehorned big American engines into small European (or European-style) chassis for many a year. Some of them, like Railton in the 1930s and Allard in the 1950s, had been pretty successful at it; others, like Briggs Cunningham with his Continentals, had failed commercially while essentially succeeding technically.

There is almost nothing complicated in putting a compact, simple production engine into a low-tech chassis. Neither is there anything particularly complicated, you might have thought, about selling it to the public. Yet without Carroll Shelby there would have been no Cobra.

Shelby was the one who was in the right place at the right time between Ford's light and lusty little engine and AC's crisp-handling but power-starved chassis. Shelby was the one with the vision, and the one with the gift of being able to deal with anyone, from the floor sweeper to the chairman of a corporation, with the same convincing Texan charm. Shelby is that totally lovable type who can sell the most unlikely sounding scheme to the most cynical of partners and only then go away and ponder how to make it work. Shelby has had the world kick him in the teeth more than once but still does not acknowledge the concept of failure.

Starting from nowhere, he did as much as anyone in the 1950s to reshape Europe's image of US motor racing, and especially of US racing drivers. He drove in Formula 1 and he won Le Mans in 1959 for Aston Martin. When his often brilliant, often cruelly unlucky racing career was prematurely ended by a recurring heart problem, he went full-steam into his dream of creating a very special sports car: the fastest sports car in the world.

He had no formal engineering training, but saw this as no obstacle at all. He had no money either, but he knew people who did – and that they happened to be one of the biggest companies in the world did not seem to intimidate him unduly.

The Cobra was his first production project of any kind. Its success led him into an extremely high-powered partnership with Ford, both on the GT40 programme and on production cars like the Shelby Mustangs, and this partnership was based almost entirely on personality.

One sentence in Wallace A. Wyss's book *Shelby's Wildlife* sums the man up beautifully:

Shelby's glamorous image – tall, gentlemanly, white teeth, California tan, cowboy hat – seemed

The hat and the smile: Carroll Shelby's high profile Texan image was one of the things that made him so marketable.

bright and promising in the drab Detroit atmosphere and Ford executives were surprised later when they asked *Hot Rod* editor Ray Brock about the extensive holdings of Mr Shelby, the Texas cattle baron, and found that Mr Shelby owned little more than his smile and his hat . . .

Mr Brock had a contribution to make to the Cobra project, too, but this came later. To understand the Cobra, you need first to go back to Shelby.

A TEXAN CHILDHOOD

Shelby was born on 11 January 1923, in Leesburg, Texas, a small town of about 200 people, some 120 miles north-east of Dallas.

Both his parents were local folk, and church-going Baptists. His father, Warren Hall Shelby, was a Texas mailman, making his deliveries by horse buggy. His mother had been born Eloise Lawrence. Carroll had a sister, Anne, three years his junior, and his family life was pretty comfortable by back-country standards – the mail paid his father reasonably well. Well enough, anyway, for him to buy his first car when Carroll was just short of five years old.

Warren Hall Shelby loved cars and he passed the affection on to Carroll, who remembered that first second-hand car as a dark green 1925 Overland tourer with a folding top, artillery wheels, a manual gearshift and a wood-rimmed steering wheel. Shelby used to watch his father tinker under the bonnet, and used to sit on his knee and hold the steering wheel.

In 1928, Shelby Senior bought a new Overland, a Whippet, with wire wheels which made a deep impression on Shelby Junior.

In 1930, the family moved to Dallas where Warren Shelby was promoted to postal clerk. Carroll graduated from high school, but only just – because his interest was elsewhere – not just in cars but in aeroplanes too.

He had started to have medical problems when he was very young, and he was quite a sickly youth for a few years. When he was around nine or ten a heart murmur was diagnosed and he had to take afternoon rests, on doctor's orders. He tired easily but he grew tall and gradually seemed to grow out of the worst of his problems.

He had learned to drive by the time he was fourteen, helped by his father and a very scruffy 1934 Dodge. He had his own car a year later, owned by his father because he was not legally old enough to own it himself. He drove a few other cars, mostly of the crash-gearbox sort, which meant he had to learn to double declutch.

His father took him to the dirt-track races

at the local 'bull-ring' ovals, too, and when his father could not take him he would go on his own, to get involved in the sort of minor fetching and carrying that has been the thin end of many a racing career wedge.

The other distraction was aeroplanes. There were lots of airfields scattered around his part of Texas and by the time he was driving, Shelby was odd-jobbing at those too, sometimes to be allowed to sit in a cockpit, eventually even for a few short rides. His first (paid for by his clearly very understanding father) was a joy ride in a Ford Trimotor and he was frightened to death.

There were motor bikes too. Carroll's first job was as a delivery rider for a local drugstore, using an Excelsior bike. After he had fallen off just one time too many, at least without major injury, he decided to stick to cars and he quit his job on the spot.

Around 1939 he met Jeanne Fields at a Baptist church social. They were married in December 1943, just after Shelby's father had died from heart trouble. Family finances at the time meant that a college career was out of the question for Carroll, and his mother was not as supportive as his father of any notions of his being a racing driver, so his love of aeroplanes led him to the military and the Army Air Corps.

INTO THE AIRFORCE

With the help of a friendly recruiting sergeant he organized a posting near to home (which meant near to mother, and wife-to-be) at Randolph Field. After basic training, his first job for the airforce was moving tons of chicken manure from an old farm to flower beds on the base. This is not just a bit of trivia – it has a bearing on the Shelby story in a few years time.

After hauling chicken manure, he drove a fire truck on the base for a few months but with the war in Europe under way, he eventually got the chance to fly. His pre-flight training started in November 1941 and in September 1942 he became a sergeant, at Ellington Field, near Houston. In his training days around Sherman, Texas, he used to fly over his fiancée's family farm. Occasionally he dropped letters and once he actually landed and took her for a joyride with her mother. Shelby was clearly never a slave to the rule book.

In December 1942, he was commissioned as a second lieutenant, and that was as far as his promotions went. He graduated to teaching new recruits to fly bombers, but he never saw active service. In fact, by the time he left the Air Corps in August 1945, the furthest he had been in his four and a half year's flying was to the Gulf of Mexico.

That does not mean that his career as pilot and instructor was uneventful. As well as his courting by aeroplane, there was also a time when he crashed during a bombing instruction run over the desert. He got his pupils out first, hung on as long as he could before he bailed out himself, and had to walk back alone across miles of nothing but desert.

By the time he had left the service, he had more or less worked the flying bug out of his system and he had no ambitions to carry on as a commercial pilot. Unfortunately, he had no training to do anything else either, so his post-war options were strictly limited.

His first son was born in November 1946, which made it essential for him to find something to pay the bills. He went into the ready-mixed concrete trucking business with a long-time friend, Bailey Gordon, starting with one truck each but soon building up a substantial business with more trucks and employing a number of drivers.

In 1947, Shelby branched out on his own with his trucks, carrying timber for the building industry. Successful as he was, he was worried by the possibility of a slump in the building business and with a little help from his oil-man father-in-law he sold out of the trucking business and went into oil, starting from the bottom during 1948 and 1949 as a roughneck, but finding that there was little money and few prospects in that side of the oil business.

That led to Shelby's most famous career outside of motor sport. Determined to be successful at something, he submitted himself to a series of aptitude tests, which, for some reason, suggested that he was best suited to working with animals.

THE FASTEST CHICKEN FARMER IN THE WORLD

At the time, chicken farming was a developing industry in Texas. Shelby had had his Air Corps experience with at least one aspect of chickens, and there was even government finance available to help him get started.

Typically, Shelby did not go for half measures. His first batch was 20,000 birds and in the first three-month cycle he made around $5000 profit. It was too good to last, though. His second batch was wiped out by disease – and his money and business went with them, sending him back to odd-jobbing for a meagre living, and raising a few pheasants and Irish setters on the farm.

With time on his hands, he got involved with cars again, more as a hobby than as a job, initially working on a friend's special. The friend was Ed Wilkins. He and Shelby had been at school together, and Wilkins now had a ladder-framed racer with flathead Ford V8 running gear and a homemade body.

In January 1952, Shelby (now father of two) raced Wilkins' flathead special in a drag race meeting at Grand Prairie Naval Airbase, Texas. Against admittedly mediocre competition, he won very easily, which pleased Wilkins so much that he gave Shelby a chance to try his hand at circuit racing, with his MG TC. His first circuit race

was in May 1952 at Norman, Oklahoma; he won his class, in an event sanctioned by the then new Sports Car Club of America (SCCA), after the early leader had spun off. Later on the same day, and still with the TC, he won another race – this time against several much more powerful Jaguar XK120s.

That was the start of Carroll Shelby's racing career. In August, he won again with a borrowed XK120 in Okmulgee, Oklahoma. In November, at Caddo Mills, Texas, he drove a Cadillac-Allard owned by wealthy sportsman Charles Brown of Monroe, Louisiana. He won, of course – this time against strong opposition including Masten Gregory, who thereafter became a lifelong friend.

Shelby drove the whole 1953 season as an amateur, almost exclusively with the fearsome Cadillac-Allards. For a while he drove for Charlie Brown, then for Roy Cherryhomes of Jacksboro, Texas. Cherryhomes paid Shelby's expenses, which was a step in the right direction, and Shelby rewarded him with nine wins from nine starts.

A Shelby trademark appeared for the first time in 1953, in a race at Eagle Mountain Naval Airbase – his striped dungarees.

I'd been working on the farm when I realized I was due to race. It was a hot day so I didn't bother to change. I found the overalls cool and comfortable and I won the race, too. I became identified with them and after that I just wore them all the time.

Even though he might have looked like a chicken farmer in the old dungarees, Shelby was now becoming quite a serious racing driver. His career took another step in January 1954 with his first race outside North America. The race was the Mil Kilometres de la Ciudad de Buenos Aires and Shelby was one of four SCCA drivers invited to take part by the Automobile Club of Argentina.

Cherryhomes supplied the familiar

The Fastest Chicken Farmer in the World, in striped dungarees, celebrates after winning Le Mans for Aston Martin in 1959. Aston patron David Brown and team driver Jack Fairman (with champagne) are on the right.

Cadillac-Allard and Shelby's running expenses, but did not go to the event himself. Shelby's co-driver was an airline pilot, Dale Duncan, who took care of the travel arrangements. Duncan also took care of putting out a carburettor fire on the car in the pits when no fire extinguisher was available. Suffice it to say that stage one of his improvised fire fighting involved climbing up onto the bonnet of the car.

Shelby and Duncan eventually finished tenth as the race was punctuated by accidents and won by a Ferrari. They won the amateur division, and with it the Kimberly Cup donated to the SCCA by Gentleman Jim Kimberly, millionaire sportsman and racing enthusiast and the Kimberly of Kimberly-Clark (makers of Kleenex).

It was Shelby's last drive in the Cherryho-

me's Allard but, more importantly, it was the race at which he was first spotted by the European who was to shape the most important phase of his racing career. That was Aston Martin race director John Wyer, and Shelby was introduced to him by works driver Peter Collins, who happened to be staying at the same hotel.

Wyer had seen and heard enough of Shelby to offer him an expenses-paid drive for Aston at Sebring, in March 1954. Shelby jumped at the chance and was well placed in the race until the rear axle broke after seventy-seven laps. Nevertheless, Sebring with Aston had given him the chance to make contacts, both European and rich American. Most important of all, Wyer invited him to Europe to drive the Aston DBR, providing he paid his own expenses.

Aston team manager John Wyer, the man who had the faith to bring Shelby to Europe, and later collaborator with the GT40.

It was not his only option at the time. He was also mulling over an offer from a west-Texan oil millionaire by the name of Guy Mabee, who had plans to build an American sports car to beat the Europeans – and this was a good eight years before the Cobra emerged!

Mabee had built a 200mph (322kph) special for his son to drive at the Bonneville speed trials in 1953 and he wanted Shelby to develop a roadgoing sports car around the same basics of tubular chassis, beam-axle front and big Chrysler V8 engine. Faced with the choice between a paid job with Mabee and the chance to go racing in Europe, Shelby (encouraged by his wife) decided to go with the Aston deal.

In fact Mabee helped Shelby finance the trip and tentatively agreed to buy an Aston

from the works for him to run in races where the team had not entered him. Shelby would also, of course, be able to pick up ideas for Mabee's own planned car.

In the end, Mabee never did buy the Aston and John Wyer, knowing the state of Shelby's finances, refused Carroll's gentlemanly but totally impracticable offer to honour the option himself.

INTO EUROPE

Meanwhile, leaving Jeanne at home and arriving in Europe in April 1954, Shelby kicked off his European racing career in a DBR3, with a second place to Duncan Hamilton at a wet Aintree meeting. On the strength of that result, he persuaded Wyer to run him at Le Mans, co-driving with journalist and racer Paul Frère. Around the 100-lap mark, Shelby drove into the pits complaining of wobbly steering, the mechanics jacked the car up and a front wheel fell off – taking its broken stub axle with it.

Shelby did rather better in the 1954 Supercortemaggiore GP at Monza. Sharing a 'semi-private' Aston with Graham Whitehead, he finished fifth overall and won $2,000, his first professional winnings and not a moment too soon, leaving a bit over even after paying his shared expenses. Soon after, in July, he finished his first European trip with third place in an Aston 1-2-3 at Silverstone, behind Collins and Roy Salvadori. Wyer was well pleased.

Having returned to the USA in August to find no future in the Mabee project, Shelby was unemployed again. This time it was Cherryhomes to the rescue, paying Shelby to drive his C-Type Jaguar in two late-season races.

Another European contact gave the next break: Donald Healey asked Shelby to go record-breaking for him at Bonneville in a team which included no less a record-breaker than former land-speed record hol-

Shelby's first race in Europe was at Aintree in April 1954, with a DBR3 in American racing colours. Shelby finished second to another future Le Mans winner, Duncan Hamilton, in the wet.

Shelby (left) with Donald Healey (right) during record runs at Bonneville. Shelby had a longstanding friendship with Healey, whom he described as a 'kindred spirit'. If BMC had been more flexible, Healey might well have built the Cobra.

der Captain George Eyston. With super-charged and unsupercharged Healey 100Ss and a special streamliner, the team took more than seventy Class D records – and Donald Healey joined the exclusive Bonne-ville 200mph (322kph) club.

That led to Shelby driving a works Healey with Roy Jackson-Moore (another of the record-breaking team) in the 1954 Carrera Panamericana road race. It was a major disaster for Shelby. He arrived too late to practise and what knowledge he had of the course was gained from driving the wrong way along the route from Mexico City to the start.

He crashed into a road marker 175km into the race, north of Oaxaca. The car went end over end and most of the passenger side, including the wheels and the metal tonneau cover, were totally torn away. Fortunately, Jackson-Moore was not sitting in it because, having already frightened each other to death just getting to the event, the drivers had agreed to fly between stints rather than passenger each other.

Shelby apologized to Donald Healey after-wards, saying that an attractive Mexican girl had caught his eye, but he couldn't have felt much like joking: he had badly shattered his arm and had to wait some seven hours for an ambulance to arrive, consoled by two Brooklyn girls who had seen the accident happen and enough local beer and Mexican brandy to take some of the pain away.

Literally adding insult to injury, the Mexican authorities then refused to let Shelby out of the country for a full week until he explained the whereabouts of two missing Austin-Healey wheels, which were on the shipping documents but, evidently, not on what little was left of the car. Even when he arrived home, he had major compli-cations with his shattered elbow and spent the next eight months either suffering operations or in casts until he was reason-ably healed.

That did not stop him racing. He was driving again by January 1955, cast and all. He developed a system of swapping to a lightweight fibreglass cast just before a race and driving with his hand taped to the steering wheel for support.

Still not fully mended, he co-drove a 3-litre Ferrari 750 Monza with future world champion Phil Hill at Sebring, and finished second to Jaguar. Shelby and Hill thought they had won, but they were placed second by just twenty-five seconds after a protest from Jaguar and eight days of checking the lap charts by the authorities. Winning the Index of Performance was not particularly consoling.

From July 1955, Shelby had a new spon-sor, Tony Paravano, an extremely wealthy west-coast construction man, racing enthu-siast and prolific buyer of Ferraris. He already had ten and decided to add maybe fifteen more. He wanted Shelby to drive them and told him that he could choose which, starting on a race-by-race arrange-ment. By September, Shelby was well estab-lished with Paravano and the two went to Europe together on one of Paravano's regu-lar Ferrari-buying outings.

AN ENCOUNTER WITH FERRARI

Good customer though he was (and good man, too, apparently – he later became a strong champion for professional drivers' rights), Paravano was not Enzo Ferrari's type. He thought nothing of modifying his Ferraris, both bodily and mechanically, and Ferrari did not think much of it. The two had a full and frank exchange of opinions and Paravano took his money down the road to Maserati, who were not quite so prima donna-ish.

It was Shelby's first direct experience of Ferrari and it set the tone for the way he always thought of him in the future: arro-gant and autocratic, the sort of man it would be very satisfying to beat with an all-American sports car.

Shelby drove all kinds of everything for Paravano through 1955, including a Formula 1 Maserati 250F in the Syracuse Grand Prix in October, where he finished sixth. He drove a Ferrari 121LM at Oulton Park, but retired; his co-driver Gino Munaron crashed their 750 Monza in the Targa Florio. He was also free to drive for others and that led to his finishing ninth overall and winning the 1,500 class in the Tourist Trophy at Dundrod, with a Porsche 550 Spyder, which he shared with his old buddy Masten Gregory.

Back in the USA, he won a race at the Seattle Seafair races with one of the Ferraris – adding to a tally of more than ten US race wins in 1955. But he ended the season just as he had ended 1954 – with a large accident at Palm Springs. This time, at least, he was unhurt, but his Ferrari was not, after climbing over the back of an Olds Special.

A big year for Shelby was 1956. From May he was driving for John Edgar, a son of the family that owned the Hobart Manufacturing Co, world-famous manufacturer of weight scales and associated equipment. Edgar was another Ferrari enthusiast, a clever investor and, later, the major backer of Riverside Raceway. Shelby also renewed his Aston Martin contact, and his first 1956 race was in the works DB3S, with Roy Salvadori at Sebring, to finish fourth.

In all he had around twenty races in 1956, mainly for Edgar in Ferraris including his 4.9-litre 375 Plus, a 2-litre Testarossa 500, a 4.4-litre 121LM, and Luigi Chinetti's ex-Formula 1, ex-Indianapolis 375, which he used to win the Mount Washington and Grant's Despair hillclimbs. He won at Pebble Beach and Fort Worth in Ferraris, but he also won some races in an Alfa Veloce special for Max Hoffman, the famous importer of anything European and sporty. Having survived some fairly desperate racing in 1956, Shelby ended the season with another accident, breaking his shoulder while playing beach football with a coconut during the Nassau speedweeks.

It had been a turning-point year. The strain of racing with little or no income was telling on his marriage, yet he was doing well enough to be named *Sports Illustrated*'s Driver of the Year – with his picture on the cover! He was making some money by tyre-testing, and doing some modest promotional work, but he really needed a proper income. He tried; during 1956 he had opened a dealership, Carroll Shelby Sports Cars, in Dallas. He was backed by Dick Hall, an oilman from Abilene, Texas and brother of Jim Hall, who later built the Chaparral sports racing cars that gave America some real success in Europe.

Shelby knew Hall through driving his Monza Ferrari in a couple of races, and they had talked about getting into the sports car sales business in Dallas where there was little or no competition. They went for European cars: MGs and Healeys as basics, Maseratis for exotica; they even sold Rolls-Royces from their premises at 5611 Yale.

Shelby was quite a well-known racer in the south west by then, and he could really have capitalized on his name but, as ever, he never found the time to devote to the business because of his racing.

He started 1957 still with John Edgar, and took second place in his Ferrari 375 Plus in the first Cuban GP, behind Juan Manuel Fangio in a Maserati 300S. In January, he had been back to Ferrari at Maranello to spend some of Edgar's money and had another argument with Ferrari himself. This was the occasion when Shelby was discussing the possibility of a works drive for Ferrari and discovered that Ferrari's idea of a working arrangement was all rather one-sided and that *Ingegnere* Ferrari clearly had no respect for Shelby's abilities. It was the point where Shelby left with the parting shot that one day he would be back to whip Ferrari's ass. Maybe it was the day the Cobra was really born.

A MIXED YEAR

Ferrari notwithstanding, 1957 was Shelby's best year as a driver, but quite a mixed one. He was disqualified from Sebring (where he was sharing a works Maserati 300S with Roy Salvadori), for refuelling too early. The possibility of a GP drive for Maserati in Europe, alongside Fangio and Stirling Moss, came to nothing, but he was very successful at home in Edgar's new 300S and 450S Maseratis. He won nineteen races and his second SCCA Championship.

It all came to a nasty end when he had a terrible crash on the first lap of practice at the inaugural Riverside meeting in September with Edgar's brand new Maserati 450. It was, he admits, a simple driver error. He survived it, but with severe back and facial injuries. He had three vertebrae fused together by his doctors and needed seventy-two stitches in his face, mainly tacking his nose back on, followed by a long haul of plastic surgery.

Incredibly though, he was back in business by November, back at Riverside and in the same car! He even won, fighting back to beat Dan Gurney's Ferrari after spinning on the first lap. As the year ended, so did his association with John Edgar and, with his marriage now over too, he started to look back towards Europe – as much, he now admits, as a means to studying sports car design as strictly for racing.

Early in 1958, he saw one of the less attractive sides of racing when he was prevented from running at Indianapolis by a rule that said two rookie drivers could not qualify in the same car. The owner of the car that was supposed to give him his Indy debut had already taken his obligatory test in the car even though he did not really intend to drive in the race, so that was the end of Shelby's chances. He explained in basic Anglo-Saxon terms what he thought of the organizers' inflexibility and never went back to Indy.

He signed up to drive for Aston again instead, but based himself in Modena and learned to speak Italian. It was not much of a year. He retired from Sebring with a broken gear linkage, took third place at Spa, retired from the Nurburgring 1,000km with a transmission problem, grabbed another third at the Goodwood Tourist Trophy, but missed the big one, Le Mans, through illness. He did manage a couple more GP outings with Maserati 250Fs for Centro Sud and Temple Buell, and his best result was fourth place in the Italian GP where he shared his car with old buddy Masten Gregory.

During 1958, he sold out of Carroll Shelby Sports Cars to the Halls, whom he remained good friends with and was happy to let use his name. He was happy enough to stay in Europe for 1959 with Aston. He drove the enterprising but unsuccessful Aston DBR4/250 F1 car as well as the Aston sports cars and he drove Temple Buell's Maserati 250F GP car again, too, but he did not achieve much in his odd GP outings against very much better cars.

SHELBY: LE MANS WINNER

This did not matter particularly since 1959 will always be remembered as the year when Shelby, in striped chicken-farmer dungarees, won Le Mans for Aston Martin and helped them to the World Sports Car Constructors' Championship.

He shared his DBR1/300 with Roy Salvadori at Le Mans and helped the team to its historic win in spite of suffering, virtually throughout the race, from dysentery. After pooling all the winnings (by prior arrangement), each of the Aston drivers at Le Mans, Shelby included, took away around $8,000 apiece. It was his biggest single pay-day.

It also led to a brief blaze of celebrity, including doing some very clean-cut adverts

Shelby drove single seaters, too, including the ambitious but ill-starred Aston GP car, here at Silverstone in 1959.

The big one: Shelby on his way to victory (and his biggest ever racing pay day) at Le Mans in June 1959. Shelby was partnered by Roy Salvadori in the Aston DBR1/300.

Shelby on the limit in his last race for Aston, with the DBR1 at Goodwood. The Tourist Trophy decided the 1959 Manufacturers' Championship; Stirling Moss took over Shelby's car after a pit fire had sidelined his own, went on to win the race, and Aston won the championship.

for Gillette, some of them dubbed into terribly English English. They were fun and they paid well, but they would not last; Shelby was still busily filing away contacts for his longer term plans as a sports car manufacturer.

By 1960, these plans were starting to dominate his thinking. It was to be his last racing season. His heart trouble was recurring with the strain of racing and general overwork. Before his heart problem was accurately diagnosed, he did some races, with medication, in a Maserati T61 Birdcage, including winning at Riverside in May and Castle Rock in June to win the USRRC Championship. He drove an amazing variety of cars through 1960, including Lance Reventlow's Scarab (which was yet another attempt to beat the Europeans with an all-American sports car).

In December, after finishing fifth in the Riverside GP with the Birdcage, Shelby retired with few regrets and the time at last

to devote to his other projects. He had moved to California to be near to the hot-rod building community where there was the talent to build his planned car. He had a small but growing Goodyear racing-tyre distributorship and some shared workshop space in Dean Moon's tuning emporium where he could work on his car when it became a bit more of a reality – an inexpensive US sports car to compete with the best Europeans, maybe the fastest sports car in the world.

Meanwhile, with a living still to earn, he was setting up the Carroll Shelby School of High Performance Driving at Riverside. He employed Pete Brock and John Timanus as instructors, who both have their part to play in the sports car story. In 1961, through his Goodyear racing-tyre connections, he was about to have a chance meeting with a Ford racing engineer who later turned out to have the key to what became the Shelby AC/ Cobra Powered by Ford.

2 AC – The Company

There is a certain irony in the fact that AC Cars, the second main element in the story of the raunchiest sports car in the world, started in the motor business not as sports car builders, but as makers of a three-wheeled delivery vehicle that looked like nothing so much as an open, motorized tricycle with a large box on the front.

The company that became AC started life in 1904 as Autocars and Accessories Ltd at West Norwood in south-east London. Their intention was to manufacture the Autocarrier, a low-cost, three-wheeled delivery truck for sale to small businesses who wanted to get away from horse and cart transport but who still could not afford a full-sized, four-wheeled delivery van.

The partners in the firm were a somewhat unlikely mixture: John Weller was a talented engineer, who had already designed a motor cycle and a technically interesting 20hp four-cylinder car that had been exhibited at the 1903 Crystal Palace Motor Show, which was just up the road from Norwood; John Portwine, who provided the £200 working capital, was the owner of a chain of butcher's shops.

The Autocarrier was simple but quite clever for its purpose. It had an air-cooled, single-cylinder 631cc engine under the rudimentary bench seat, driving the single rear wheel by a chain. A two-speed epicyclic gear and the clutch were incorporated in the hub. There was tiller steering and no bodywork other than big cycle-type mudguards, plus the carrying box, which sat between the two front wheels.

It wasn't the sort of vehicle to say that its makers had any great sporting ambitions, but it sold well to domestic customers including the well-known stores Selfridges and Maples, to Associated Newspapers in Fleet Street and to the Great Western Railway Company. It was even exported as far as China and Argentina.

AC – AND INTO PASSENGER CARS

In 1907, the company was renamed Auto Carriers Ltd, and the famous AC initials thus appeared. In 1908, Weller and Portwine went into the passenger car business, not with Weller's advanced 20hp car but with a passenger-carrying version of the Autocarrier, which they called the AC Sociable, with basketwork 'bodywork' and the driver sitting behind, perched on a motorcyle-type saddle.

Later versions sat the driver and passenger side by side in 'forecar'-type bodywork, but still retained the tiller steering. The Sociable stayed in production until 1914 and the outbreak of World War I. It, and the delivery wagon, managed to turn Auto Carriers into a very substantial company, reorganized in 1911 as Auto Carriers (1911) Ltd with capital increased to £25,000. The expansion also brought about a move in 1911 to bigger premises at Thames Ditton, Surrey, where AC stayed until the early 1980s before growing losses triggered an even more than usually turbulent era in the company's history.

Just before the war, in 1913, Auto Carriers showed that they did have serious passenger car ambitions when they launched their first four-wheeler light car. It was designed by Weller, of course, and used a

THE A.C. TRICAR.

Modest beginnings for a sports car builder: the Tricar developed directly from the Autocarrier delivery van.

proprietary engine, the French-made 10hp, 1094cc four-cylinder Fivet. It showed the spark of Weller's imagination in having its three-speed, aluminium-cased gearbox in unit with the back axle, and incorporating a disc transmission brake.

Like the Sociable, the pretty and sporty four-wheeler was a victim of the outbreak of war, after less than 100 had been built. Even without them, though, AC expanded considerably, principally making shells and fuses for the military.

The first post-war AC model was announced in October 1918, even before the war was officially over, if only by a couple of weeks. Predictably, it was little more than an updated version of the pre-war car. It went into production in 1919, briefly with a larger version of the Fivet engine, but then, as supplies of the engine from the Billancourt factory dried up, AC switched to the 1.5-litre four-cylinder 11.9hp Anzani unit, as used later to power another famous British sporting car – the chain-drive Frazer-Nash.

Even in the Tricar days, AC had a sporting bent.

Early days in West Norwood under the famous initials that first appeared during 1907. The company was growing fast.

The 1913 10hp was AC's first four-wheeler. It reappeared after World War I at the beginning of a chain of company connections that stretched right to the Cobra.

Selwyn Francis Edge (in the car) helped AC survive through hard times in the 1920s, and promoted its sporting image to the full, but almost saw the company die.

THE LONG LINK TO THE COBRA

The connections are interesting. AC's initial order of 2,000 engines came at a very opportune moment for the struggling British Anzani company who made them and, on the strength of it, Weller and Portwine became directors of British Anzani. They stayed on the AC and Anzani boards until September 1922 when they were replaced by new AC directors S. F. Edge, Lt.-Col. John S. Napier and Thomas Gillett.

Edge transferred production of the Anzani engine to his Cubitt factory (which also

made bodywork for AC cars) but never did complete the initial order of 2,000 engines to AC. He did, however, begin to supply the Anzani engine to the new Frazer-Nash company, founded in November 1922, just down the road from AC in Kingston, Surrey.

Frazer-Nash built exceedingly sporty cars; in 1927, the company became known as AFN Ltd and later came under the control of H. J. Aldington, and his brother, Bill. In 1934, Aldington obtained British sales and manufacturing rights to BMW cars, and began to import several models to be sold here as Frazer-Nashes. Among them was the classic BMW 328 sports car (sold as the

Frazer-Nash 328), which had a brilliant but complex overhead-valve, six-cylinder engine designed by one Fritz Fiedler.

During World War II, Aldington's brother D. A. Aldington was in the army. He worked in the Ministry of Supply and came into contact with the Bristol Aeroplane Company. When Bristol went into car manufacture at the end of the war, they gained H. J. Aldington as a director and, through Aldington, acquired the drawings and tooling for the BMW 328 engine, as war reparations. They also gained Fritz Fiedler himself, whom Aldington had helped free from internment.

Bristol produced a vastly improved version of the already brilliant horizontal-pushrod engine, mainly by improving the metallurgy and the build quality, and went on to build up an enviable reputation as a very high-class sporting car maker. Bristol also supplied what had now become 'their' six-cylinder engine to several other British sporting marques, especially for racing, where it could be persuaded to give extraordinarily high power outputs. And that, of course, was the six-cylinder Bristol engine that AC adopted for the AC Ace, to supplement their own ageing six, in 1956.

The final twist that led directly to the Cobra was that supplies of the Bristol engine, to AC as well as to anyone else, only dried up after Bristol switched to using a big American V8 – the 313cu in (5,133cc) Chrysler – for the 1961 407.

So the highly refined 407 beat the Cobra into production as a successful hybrid, but at the same time opened the door for the Cobra itself to evolve.

AN ENGINE THAT RAN AND RAN

Incredibly, the engine that AC supplemented with the six-cylinder Bristol for the Ace essentially dated back to a time even before the Anzani episode that started the chain just described. It was AC's own six-cylinder, and the original was designed by John Weller as a 1,496cc unit, way back in 1919.

It started with 35bhp and by its final appearance in the Ace it had risen to 103bhp. The capacity had gone up to 1,992cc (and power to 40bhp) in 1922 and that is where it stayed until it finally went out of production late in 1963, *after* the Cobra had been launched!

As we shall see later, it was actually a very good engine, and its main contribution to this story is that, in spite of the company to all intents and purposes dying in the meantime, it gradually turned AC into a very sporty manufacturer. The other main influence that brought that about was the change of directors mentioned earlier.

By the time Selwyn Francis Edge joined the board of AC in February 1921, he was one of Britain's most celebrated motor industry figures. He is generally credited with 'inventing' the six-cylinder engine (not the AC six-cylinder engine, but the six-cylinder engine as a genre). That was in 1903.

Australian-born Edge had arrived in England in 1871, aged three, grown up to become a famous racing and record-breaking cyclist and moved inexorably into racing cars, importing them and finally manufacturing them. he is also credited with being the British motor industry's first real public relations manager, promoting everything he did with a rare fervour.

The six-cylinder engine concept appeared in the 1903 Napier, made by the company with which Edge had a close but finally acrimonious business relationship, which ended around 1912 with an agreement on Edge's part to stay out of the motor industry for seven years. Seven years as a pig-breeder and a career as Controller of Agricultural Machinery to the Ministry of Munitions kept him busy until he bought his way into AC in 1921.

Weller and Portwine had already shown their enthusiasm for sporting competition, and Edge was an even firmer believer in motor sport as a means of promotion. Thomas Gillett was an accomplished competition driver who was particularly active in AC's record-breaking activities.

A SPORTING REPUTATION

By this time, AC was a big company with 900 employees and capital of £330,000. Edge promised a string of competition successes with both the four- and six-cylinder models, from record-breaking runs at Brooklands (conveniently close to the doorstep, of course) and Montlhèry (a bit further away, on the outskirts of Paris), to many wins in races, hillclimbs and reliability trials, and in rallies.

Weller developed a number of four-cylinder engine variants for the record-breakers, including overhead-camshaft eight- and sixteen-valve units. In 1921, Harry Hawker, of the famous aviation family, used a special version of Weller's 1.5-litre engine in a single-seater chassis to lap Brooklands at over 100mph (161kph), and Kaye Don also set 100mph (161kph) production car records at Brooklands in 1922. A six-cylinder AC set a world 24-hour record of 82.6mph (133kph) at Montlhèry in 1925 and another took records for up to 15,000 miles (24,135km) (in spite of overturning and losing 15 hours for repairs) in December 1927.

That car was driven by the Hon Victor Bruce (another of the great British sporting motorists), and Mrs Bruce. In 1926 the Hon Victor, with W. J. Brunell, had also used a six-cylinder AC to win the Monte Carlo Rally – the first time a British car had ever

AC director Thomas Gillett en route *to breaking the 24-hour record at Montlhèry in 1925 with a streamlined six-cylinder single-seater AC racer.*

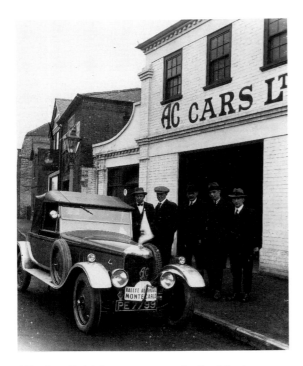

The first British car ever to win the Monte: the winner, the Hon Victor Bruce (second from right), shows off the six-cylinder 1926 rally winner outside the Thames Ditton works.

won the event, and the only time it was ever won from the far-flung starting point of John o' Groats.

In spite of the competition successes, though, and in spite of the fact that AC had some really quite good cars in the early 1920s, like the Montlhèry Six Sports, the company was going through severe financial and political traumas.

There were internal disagreements between the new directors and Weller and Portwine, especially over the non-fulfilment of the Anzani engine contract, and that contributed to British Anzani going into liquidation in 1925. Weller and Portwine had already left both the AC and Anzani boards, in September 1922. That left control to Edge, as Chairman and Governing Direc-

tor. Also in 1922, the company name was changed from the rather clumsy Auto Carriers (1911) Ltd to the simpler AC Cars Ltd.

Edge did everything he possibly could to help AC and but for him the company could easily have gone out of business completely in the mid-1920s. At that point, Vauxhall Motors (with a history of sporting models of their own) were a substantial shareholder in AC, but about to be absorbed into General Motors in October 1925. With Vauxhall having their own financial problems in the slump years of the mid-1920s, GM probably had very little interest in propping up their acquired interest in AC. Edge bought all Vauxhall's 80,000 shares in AC, increasing his own total investment in the company to £135,000.

In spite of their competition successes, though, AC's problem was that they were steadily falling behind the production opposition, probably because they just couldn't afford to keep up. Sporty as the cars were, front-wheel brakes were still only an option until as late as 1927, and AC only offered three-speed gearboxes right up to 1933. The four-cylinder model hardly sold at all and went out of production in 1927 after having absorbed too much money for too long.

The company itself was restructured again in 1927 with the formation of a new company, AC (Acedes) Ltd. That company went into liquidation in 1929 when Edge and Gillett, both having lost their substantial investments, left. Car production stopped and all that remained was the service department, which produced two six-cylinder AC engines to drive the generators on the R101 airship.

THE HURLOCK ERA

In 1930, the virtually redundant Thames Ditton factory was bought by brothers Charles and William Hurlock. The Hurlocks did not intend to revive AC car production;

they wanted to use the works as a depot for their existing business – selling and servicing cars and commercial vehicles from a base in Brixton, south-east London. Charles, and William's son Derek, were the Hurlocks who eventually had the vision, some thirty years on, to listen to a tall Texan by the name of Carroll Shelby when he offered them an American V8 engine to turn their little Ace sports car into something he wanted to call the Cobra.

AC crept back to a life as a car manufacturer from the time that the service manager at the surviving part of the company assembled a car for William Hurlock. Hurlock liked his AC and told enough friends that he liked it for AC to start a small run of cars again in the early 1930s, each one built to a definite order from the parts remaining in stock.

While fully aware of the limitations of the existing chassis, and particularly the badly outdated three-speed transmission, William Hurlock realized that in Weller's six-cylinder engine (by now up to 66bhp in sporting triple-carburettor form) he had the basis of a fine car. By 1933, they had such a car to take to the Motor Show at Olympia.

From there, the car-building side of the company grew fairly quickly, though never to the old levels, with a pre-war workforce barely one tenth its early 1920s peak and a total output of less than 650 cars between the resumption of production and the interruption of World War II.

Of necessity, most parts were bought in from outside suppliers. AC fitted Weller's overhead-cam six-cylinder engine, now in unit with a four-speed ENV gearbox, into a Standard 16 chassis and clothed it in their own bodywork in several different styles, including two- and four-door saloons, coupes, tourers, and a short-wheelbase sports car. AC also offered the option of a Wilson pre-selector gearbox from 1934 and a syncromesh box from 1935. Some famous names appeared on the cars of this period,

too, like Ace and Acedes, Aceca and Greyhound. They were quality cars, in the higher medium-price range, and invariably very handsome. While starting with a standard body/chassis combination to keep costs under control, AC offered customers a vast range of options – mechanical and trim – to personalize every car.

SPORTING REVIVAL

Like Edge, Weller and Portwine before them, the Hurlock brothers were firm motor sport enthusiasts, in their case mostly for rallying. In 1933 an all-girl team of AC sports tourer drivers led by Kitty Brunell, daughter of the 1926 Monte co-winner, won the RAC Rally and, in 1935, T. V. Selby narrowly failed to give AC another Monte Carlo Rally win.

In the Arnott supercharged UBS- and UBSS-engined 16/80 and 16/90 sports cars, introduced in 1937 in long and short wheelbases, Weller's faithful old six gave as much as 95bhp, and these were very useful 'off-the-shelf' competition cars. By 1937, AC were among the first British manufacturers to export to America, and they exhibited at that year's New York Show.

The outbreak of World War II in September 1939 stopped car production again as the company switched to war production. AC's wartime output was nothing if not varied, ranging through bodywork for Ford and Bedford fire trucks, fire-pump trailers, glider undercarriages, flamethrowers and six-pounder guns. They also began to make aeroplane parts for Fairey Aviation, starting an association which lasted well beyond the war.

Such ongoing contracts were enough to delay AC's return to car manufacture until late in 1947. Yet again, they used the old but good Weller engine, this time in rather nice-looking two- and four-door saloon options. Late in 1949, AC introduced the Buckland

By the late 1930s, AC were reasonably healthy again and producing sporting gems like this handsome 1938 16/80, but the sporting reputation was due to slip.

A very faithful servant: Weller's classic six-cylinder AC engine, introduced way back in 1919, is seen here in three-carburettor form in a late-1930's 16/80. It survived until 1963 – after the Cobra was launched!

Post-war mainstream was the good-looking 2-litre saloon, in two- or four-door options, not terribly quick with the old AC six but typically sporting British, none the less.

The Buckland sports tourer was in effect an open-topped 2-litre saloon, and the trail to the Ace (and finally the Cobra) started with its body builder, Ernie Bailey.

sports tourer, which, along with the saloons, sold in steadily decreasing numbers until the late 1950s.

The problem was that AC's sporting reputation was slipping badly by this stage and the opposition was getting stronger, particularly from the likes of Jaguar. Nice as the 2-litre saloons were, what was underneath was getting pretty long in the tooth by now. Weller's engine was one thing, and still well able to hold its own, but the saloon's chassis had the same non-independent, cart-spring suspension that had served ACs since well before the war, while the competition was getting well into its more sophisticated postwar stride by 1950.

Financially, the poor sales of the cars were not the end of the world for AC since, by this time, they had several other profitable strings to their bow. For one thing, the Fairey Aviation contracts were still large and ongoing. For another, in the 1950s AC had won a huge contract from the Ministry of Pensions to build glassfibre-bodied three-wheeler invalid carriages whose ugly pale-blue bodywork became a familiar sight throughout Britain, although they eventually came to be regarded as a wholly wrong approach to invalid mobility, from the points of view of both safety and dignity. AC also made an 'able-bodied' two-seater version of the 250cc Villiers-engined three-wheeler, known as the Petite, and somehow managed to sell some 2,000 examples of this dreadful contrivance up to the late 1950s.

Then there were the 'Bag Boy' electric golf

AC would never have survived on its conventional car output in the early 1950s, but huge government contracts for the controversial invalid car kept the company afloat.

AC Petite was little more than a mainstream production version of the invalid car, made alongside the Ace!

carts, made under licence from the USA, and the four electric trains that stayed in service on Southend Pier right up to 1979. All of these – invalid car, Petite, trains and Bag Boys – were made at a factory called Taggs Island, which AC had taken on in 1940, for war work.

Notwithstanding the slip in sporting image engendered by the majority of this output, AC were doing well under the Hurlocks. In October 1951 they became a public company, increasing capital by a £50,000 issue of one-shilling shares. Since the war, AC had been averaging over £50,000 a year profit.

ENTER THE ACE

The big change in image, back to being a real sports car manufacturer, came in 1953 with the launch of the second-generation Ace, the Cobra's direct ancestor.

Like many of the better things in life, the Ace – and hence, ultimately, the Cobra – grew out of a happy series of coincidences. For the Ace, the coincidences started with a place called Buntingford, in Hertfordshire, where the aluminium bodies for the Buckland tourer were made by a company called the Buckland Body Works, run by Ernie Bailey.

Just down the road from Ernie Bailey's' small works was a sports car maker called John Tojeiro. In between building his own specials, Tojeiro helped pay the bills by painting some of Bailey's newly bodied AC Bucklands in a barn which he rented from a local garage owner, Vin Davison.

To cut a long story short, Tojeiro developed a strong, lightweight tubular chassis with all-round independent suspension,

LOY 500, Cliff Davis's Bristol-engined Tojeiro, seen here at Silverstone leading a similarly powered Frazer-Nash, was one of the direct catalysts for the Ace.

mainly for racing. He sold several examples of the chassis into which customers fitted a variety of engines and around which they draped an equally catholic variety of bodies. One of the nicest of these Tojeiro specials was built for Cliff Davis, early in 1953, and registered LOY 500. It had a Bristol six-cylinder engine and a beautifully simple body that was virtually a straight copy of the Ferrari 166 Barchetta, not to mention a previous Davis car, JOY 500, of which more anon.

Davis had endless racing successes with LOY 500, and suggested to Tojeiro that the two of them should put it into some sort of production. They did not do that, but a very similar Tojeiro car owned by Vin Davison was eventually shown to AC, via Ernie Bailey. AC bought the rights, modified the shape just enough to avoid shouts of plagiarism from Maranello, and launched it at the 1953 Earls Court Motor Show as the new Ace. With, you guessed it, the Weller six-cylinder AC engine.

It was enough. The Ace was an instant success, as quick and sharp handling as it was beautiful. Production started slowly but racing successes came fast, and virtually overnight AC were known as a sports car builder again.

The story of the development of the Ace, its variants, its racing and production career and the way it evolved into the Cobra, is told in detail in a later chapter, but suffice it to say here that it was a turning point. It stayed in production from 1953 until 1964 – after the Cobra had gone into production. It went through AC, Bristol and tuned Ford engine phases, and it was the fact that the Ace was looking for another engine at the very moment when Shelby was looking for a car that made the Cobra happen.

A COMPANY ON THE EDGE

As for AC the company, the rest of the 1950s, the whole of the 1960s, and more or less everything up to the present day has been a mixture of success and knife-edged brinkmanship. They certainly did not get

The Ace, the direct ancestor of the Cobra and surely one of the most beautiful sports cars ever built. This is a Bristol-engined car at Brands Hatch in 1959, with aerodynamic tweaks of grille fairing and a racing 'screen'.

A letterhead from the late 1950s suggests what was keeping the company going at the time. Shelby obviously did not read the line that says 'All communications to be addressed to the company and not to individuals'.

The Bristol engine, seen here in a 1959 Greyhound, was derived from a pre-war BMW unit and kept AC going even after Bristol had stopped using it themselves.

rich on the Ace, its coupe sister the Aceca (launched in 1954), the Cobra, nor on the Cobra's short-lived 'European' successor, the Frua-bodied AC 428 (a luxury car far from the Cobra mould in spite of the mechanical similarities). The often ridiculed but undoubtedly lucrative invalid-car business stopped abruptly in 1976 with new safety legislation, and thereafter the company was really surviving only on building commercial trailers, and bodywork for other people's vehicles.

The 428 went out of production in 1973 after only eighty-six coupes and convertibles had been built; in the end, it was a victim of the 'energy crisis'. For most of the rest of the 1970s and much of the 1980s – even, in fact, into the 1990s – there was always a possibility that AC might become a sports car manufacturer again; it was certainly what Derek Hurlock would have liked, but it only happened in a very limited way as the company limped from one commercial crisis to another, always seemingly so close to success, yet always so far away.

The basis of the 1970's and 1980's sports-car project was a mid-engined coupe, the Diablo, built originally as a one-off prototype by Peter Bohanna and Robin Stables. With the unlikely power source of an Austin

Maxi engine and gearbox behind the cockpit, it appeared first in 1972. Derek Hurlock might have seen in the Diablo the 1972 equivalent of Tojeiro's forerunner of the Ace, but this time it just did not work out.

AC did take on the project, redesigned the car around a 3-litre Ford V6 engine and their own five-speed gearbox, turned it into quite a nice-looking little two-seater and launched it as the AC ME3000 at the 1982 London Motorfair, but they could never quite turn it into a commercially viable proposition.

The problems are irrelevant here in detail, but they revolved around gaining Type Approval (not one of the mountains the

AC's own offering on the coil-spring chassis was the AC 428, styled by Frua in Italy and a lot less rabid than the spartan Cobra, but never a great success in oil-crisis days.

The Aceca was simply a fixed-head Ace coupe. Aside from the racing Daytonas, there was never a Cobra coupe, although there were early plans to include one.

Cobra had to climb), hanging on to a disintegrating dealer network with nothing to sell, and simply making the car work properly. It did go into production of a sort during 1979, but only sixty-eight examples were sold up to 1984, by which time AC was on the rocks once again.

The rights to the ME3000, including the right to use the AC name and logo, were sold to a Scottish-based company run by one David McDonald, which became AC Cars (Scotland) Ltd. Production moved to a new factory at Hillington, Glasgow, and a few more cars began to emerge during 1984 and 1985, redeveloped by highly respected one-

time BRM engineer Aubrey Woods, as the ME2500 with Alfa-Romeo V6 power.

Unfortunately, the money ran out for AC (Scotland), too, in 1985. The project was rescued by a former Ford works racing driver turned successful marketing director, John Parsons. With Woods staying on in charge of design, the company moved back to Knebworth, Hertfordshire, as AC (Ecosse), with Parsons as chief executive. The car was relaunched in June 1989 as the Ecosse Signature with 2-litre Fiat turbo engine but there was the usual problem of trying to find the money needed to finance proper large scale production.

The mid-engined ME3000 should have been AC's production car for the 1970s and 1980s, but it had a complicated life both technically and politically, in parallel with AC themselves.

AC MKIV AND THE FORD SAGA

AC Cars (Scotland) Ltd were not the only company allowed to use the AC name and logo, and the other one has direct relevance to the Cobra story.

Briefly, for now, Brian Angliss was a devoted Cobra enthusiast by the early 1970s. He had started with a restoration business, discovered that restoring a Cobra was hampered by lack of parts availability, and started making his own. He then went into business as Cobra Parts (or CP), supplying them to other people. CP eventually made enough Cobra items to build complete cars, something far more than the often exceedingly tacky 'replicas', but a bit less than genuine Cobras (except occasionally when they were recreated around an otherwise unrestorable original, and more importantly, its numbers).

By 1980, Brian Angliss was building cars in a short series – Angliss originals, not meant to be passed off as Cobras – and things developed from there. The story is told in more detail later but, essentially, Angliss's company, CP Autokraft as it had become (and then just Autokraft), acquired most of the original Cobra jigs and tooling

Both the AC and Cobra names have survived into the 1990s with the AC MkIV, built by Brian Angliss on original jigs to pretty much the original Cobra philosophy.

from AC Cars Ltd, and also the rights to use the AC name and logo and to build Cobra-type cars, for twenty-five years, starting in 1982.

In 1984, Ford accepted the cars into their dealer network, but only half-heartedly, and helped Angliss to get the car through the Type Approval process – also supplying power trains to order. In 1987, Ford even authorized Angliss to use the Cobra name and emblem on his AC MkIVs everywhere except in the USA, where that would have made product liability devolve to Ford themselves.

Having bought out what remained of AC Cars Ltd, and therefore having rights to the name, Angliss also hatched plans to build a new, high-tech, four-wheel-drive, Ford-powered AC Ace, which was shown in prototype form at the 1986 Motor Show in Birmingham. Then, in October 1987, Ford bought a controlling, 51 per cent share in AC Cars Ltd for around £1.3 million. Angliss was delighted; AC enthusiasts were delighted. Ford revealed plans to build a turbocharged four-cylinder Cosworth-engined update of the new Ace, putting in a lot of work on a major redesign, and AC Cars moved into the new 70,000sq ft factory on the Brooklands estate.

And then, out of the blue on 22 May 1990, Ford applied for the liquidation of AC Cars, because of what they called 'a stalemate' between themselves, Brian Angliss and the company who were expected to assemble the Ace in volume. Brian Angliss, not surprisingly, announced he would fight the liquidation application.

It was sad to see the possibility of the AC name finally dying at the hands of the corporation that gave it its greatest glories with the Cobra. On the other hand, Brian Angliss was absolutely determined to carry on with the MkIV; it would not be that easy to kill off the Cobra itself.

3 The Ace

The 1953 British Motor Show at Earls Court, London, was dubbed by the press 'The 100mph Motor Show'. There were at least twenty cars in the show that would better the magic 'ton', from the sensational new Jaguar XK120 and the Triumph TR2 to the Aston Martin DB2/4 and the Allard J2X, from the Austin Healey 100-4 to the Alfa 1900. Alongside them, and attracting as much praise as any, was a new car from AC – the Ace.

It was quite some time since the launch of a new AC model had caused any real excitement beyond the ranks of the marque's faithful. AC's image had long ago slipped from sporting to staid, and no one was really expecting any changes now.

How wrong they were. There were two Ace exhibits on the stand, a complete car and a bare rolling chassis. The car was extremely handsome, the glossily-presented chassis was simple but clever. Other than the much more expensive Lagonda 3-litre, the new Ace was the only British car on show to feature all-round independent suspension.

A little over eight years later, in April 1962, the same chassis layout, give or take a few tweaks, and the same supremely elegant shape but for a couple of new swoops, would be back on a show stand (in New York) with a new engine (the lightweight Ford 260cu in (4,264cc) V8) and a new name: Shelby AC/Cobra.

In between, the Ace (which was still in production when the Cobra took its bow) had gone from AC six-cylinder to Bristol six-cylinder to Ford six-cylinder power. The switch from English Ford six-cylinder to US Ford V8 was prompted by Carroll Shelby and seized on just as eagerly by AC as they had seized on the makings of the Ace in the first place, from John Tojeiro.

The line from Ace to Cobra is as direct as that, and although the changes under the skin were actually more radical than they might have seemed at first glance, without the Ace there would have been no Cobra.

Back in 1953, the car that put AC back on the sports car map, and eventually led straight to the Cobra, was a supreme piece of opportunism. AC's own part in it was really very small, and the whole project had happened in weeks rather than long months.

OFF THE SHELF

AC managed that because they effectively bought the Ace, off the shelf, from novice racing driver and sports car builder John Tojeiro. In 1950, John Tojeiro, Portuguese-born, British-domiciled, was driving a re-bodied MG TA lightweight special, which he had rebuilt from a burned-out near wreck, but he was not doing particularly well with it. He could not afford more power and the non-independent chassis that he was stuck with was not even making the best of what he had, and he was frightening himself by having to try too hard. So Tojeiro set out to build a new chassis of his own that would be simple, easily adapted to other engines, inexpensive to build, but with the handling to make up for lack of power.

He started by building a couple of box-frame chassis along lines similar to contemporary Coopers that he had studied, but then decided to progress to a tubular chassis – not an exotic and expensive multi-tubular spaceframe but something a bit more basic and easier to build and mend.

Having acquired, as he puts it, 'a couple of lengths of pipe', he designed a simple ladder-frame of three 3in-diameter alloy steel tubes, two running longitudinally and only about a foot and a half apart, with the other linking them across the centre. The resulting H shape was bridged at its open ends by two steel box-sections, fabricated from twelve-gauge sheet. The boxes gave the frame rigidity and provided the mounting points for the suspension, the steering and the final drive unit.

The suspension was all-independent, with simple tubular lower wishbones and transverse leaf springs, front and rear. In that respect, it was very similar to the original Fiat 500 Topolino. It was also similar to the suspension on one of the Coopers that Tojeiro had looked at – another MG-powered car, built by Lionel Leonard.

Leonard was a successful club racer in the late 1940s and early 1950s, especially with a car registered JOY 500. JOY 500 seems to have had a strange gestation. It reportedly began life in 1949 as a rear-engined single-seater Cooper with a JAP 1100 engine, but by 1951 Leonard had somehow converted it into a front-engined sports car with a 1250

JOY 500, Lionel Leonard's MG TF-engined Cooper sports car, was the inspiration for John Tojeiro's ladder frames with transverse leaf suspension, which formed the basis of the Ace, and hence the Cobra. Cliff Davis bought JOY 500 from Leonard to run alongside his Tojeiro-chassised LOY 500.

Ferrari's handsome and effective 'barchetta' bodywork, from the 1949 Le Mans winning 166, gave Leonard and Davis, amongst others, something to copy. Looking at its 1949 contemporaries here, you can see why.

MG TD engine. He had given it a body that was a close copy of the Carrozzeria Touring shape of the Ferrari 166 Barchettas, which finished first and second at Le Mans in 1949.

Even though it used some familiar elements, Tojeiro's tubular ladder-frame chassis in its entirety was not a copy of anything; it was a simple but clever original. Basically, it was intended to offset any lack of power by minimal weight and fine handling. It also made full use of readily available running gear, including rack-and-pinion steering derived from the Morris Minor, Morris hubs, an ENV/Jaguar back axle, Girling dampers, Alfin cast-alloy drum brakes and Turner alloy wheels.

Even before 'Toj' had finished his first tubular chassis, let alone tested it, he had sold it. He sold it to Chris Threlfall, a young Cambridge student, who subsequently raced it with an MG engine successfully enough to attract the attention of a number of other customers. Brian Lister (later a racing car manufacturer in his own right) bought one and apparently fitted it with a JAP vee-twin engine, while Chris Sears took the Lea-Francis engine from a Frazer-Nash for his example.

SELLING THE IDEA

In 1952, another of the Tojeiro chassis was sold to Cliff Davis, an experienced and successful club racer, who had previously bought an MG Magnette-based special from the aforementioned Lionel Leonard, and had then bought Leonard's Cooper-MG, JOY 500. Leonard had sold JOY 500 in frustration after one of its frequent engine failures. By the Easter 1953 Goodwood race meeting, Cliff Davis had turned his Tojeiro chassis into a stablemate for JOY 500, appropriately registered LOY 500.

JOY 500 when owned by Cliff Davis. The simplicity is obvious, as are the Ferrari lines in the aluminium shell.

Tojeiro-chassised LOY 500, with a Bristol engine, a barchetta-style body by Eric Gray, and the flamboyant Davis at the wheel at Goodwood in 1953.

He had the car bodied by Eric Gray in Hammersmith, west London, over a lightweight tubular superstructure – Superleggera style. It looked virtually identical to the ex-Leonard Cooper-MG, with the same ersatz Ferrari 166 lines, but Davis had chosen the 2-litre Bristol six-cylinder engine to power this example.

Davis, a larger-than-life London car dealer with a reputation for his wild parties and wildly entertaining driving style, won first time out with his Tojeiro-Bristol, and went on winning fairly regularly throughout 1953, using both JOY and LOY.

Davis, with the car dealer's eye to any opportunity to sell, suggested to Tojeiro that the two of them go into partnership to build and market the car on a bigger scale. He even made a preliminary announcement of availability, in *Autosport* magazine. Tojeiro, however, was maybe less ambitious, maybe just content at the time to carry on building one-offs as he always had. Then, though, came one of those twists in the tale where coincidence shapes the future.

Tojeiro's small works were at Buntingford, mid-way between London and Cambridge, and just down the road from Ernie Bailey's Buckland coachworks, which built the bodies for the AC Buckland. Tojeiro painted some of the AC bodies for Bailey, in the old barn which he rented from another local garage owner, Vin Davison.

Davison became another Tojeiro owner, fitting his example with a Lea-Francis engine and bodywork which had the familiar 'Barchetta' egg-crate nose but a rather swoopier profile, dipping down through the doorline and sweeping up over the rear wheels – almost exactly like the Ace and Cobra that were to follow.

Where Davis had failed to convince Tojeiro to turn manufacturer, Ernie Bailey put Tojeiro in touch with a different possibility. AC Management were, of course, occasional visitors to Bailey's works and, not surprisingly, came to hear of Tojeiro's offerings.

The rather staid image of AC's output at the time did not mean that the Hurlocks had lost interest in sporting cars – far from it – but they did not have either the technical or financial resources at the time to start from scratch, as they would really have to do in order to come up with anything modern and exciting.

They were well aware, though, that the market for truly sporting cars was increasing enormously, especially in the USA, in tandem with growing post-war prosperity. If the right design happened along from an outside source, and at the right price, they would be very happy to take it on.

That was how the Hurlocks, Charles and his nephew Derek, son of William, came to be shown Vin Davison's Tojeiro-Lea Francis, and also, in the simplest terms, how the Ace was born.

BUYING THE BASICS

AC started by studying Tojeiro's design with a view to adapting it for production, and the Hurlocks also started talking financial arrangements with the designer. Eventually, that led to Tojeiro accepting a small lump sum for the chassis and body designs, plus a royalty of £5 on each car subsequently built by AC, up to the first 100 cars. In return, of course, he would help AC turn the racing chassis into a production chassis.

The Hurlocks and their own Polish-born designer, Z. T. Marcewski, had the chance to try Vin Davison's car on the road sometime in the middle of 1953, only a few months before the approaching Motor Show. Marczewski, unlike the Hurlocks, was sceptical until Tojeiro took him out for a ride in Davison's car.

Tojeiro remembers this occasion:

I motored down to Thames Ditton and showed the car to their management, including the chief designer Charles Hurlock, a dry character, who

*Vin Davison's Tojeiro, LER 371, became the first Ace prototype and show car
in one. It already has slight visual differences from the Ferrari clones and, apart
from the nose and tail, is very similar to the production Ace. Davison went to
AC to develop the car for the 1953 Motor Show.*

said 'we couldn't build this here; you'd need all
sorts of special machinery and modern welding
equipment and so on'. To which Ernie Bailey
replied, 'I can tell you that that car was built in
a place that probably isn't as big as your toilets!'

Anyway, they had a good look at it and I think
they were a bit impressed; but the designer, a
very clever man without a doubt, had his own
ideas on such things. I think he looked at it and
thought 'what a flimsy little thing this is'.
Anyhow, they said 'take him for a ride', so I
whipped him up the Kingston by-pass and we had
a bit of fun.

The welcoming committee was outside the
works when we got back and Charles Hurlock
said to Marczewski, 'well, what do you think of
it?' 'It was an experience', he replied. That's all
he said; I shall never forget it . . .

In fact Marczewski may have been shaken
by the demonstration but he came back
willing to concede that in the Tojeiro chassis
the Hurlocks had found the basis for their
new car. It was pretty well sorted out
already through racing, reliable in long-
distance races as well as quick in sprints.
For AC, it should be easier and cheaper to
build than their existing and outdated
offerings, and it would be readily adaptable
to other power units.

With virtually no time to spare, the work
that followed was all based on Davison's car,
originally registered LER 371, and Davison
was given a job at AC as a development
engineer, to work on turning his own car

John Tojeiro (born 1923)

The man who designed the chassis that led to the Ace and ultimately to the Cobra, once modestly attributed a degree of his success to his unusual surname: 'I well remember', he says, 'Roy Salvadori coming up to me at a race meeting in 1953 and saying "you'll be all right, nobody will forget that name!"'

John Tojeiro was born in Estoril, Portugal, in 1923. His mother was English and his father was a Portuguese banker whom she had fallen in love with while she was on holiday!

After his father died, John's mother brought him back to England in the 1930s, where he developed his interest in all things mechanical in the traditional way, through model cars and Meccano. After school and before the war, he started an engineering apprenticeship with a commercial vehicle manufacturer in Hertfordshire.

He bought his first motor cycle while he was in his teens, and had already had his first car before he joined the Fleet Air Arm during World War II, when it was back to a motor bike while he was working on flying boats in a training squadron on the South coast.

After leaving the services in 1946, he went back to his engineering training, and was married in 1947, but he was already trying to think of a way of earning a living connected with cars. He started to buy and sell second-hand cars, repairing and refurbishing them where necessary and learning as he went along. He also caught the racing bug. He bought an MG TA, badly fire damaged, and gave it a special lightweight body. Unfortunately, although he now knew quite a successful local MG tuner in the person of Harry Leicester, Tojeiro did not do much to improve the notoriously flexible MG's chassis and so spent a lot of his racing time frightening himself with the car's wayward handling.

Then he decided to build his own chassis, borrowing from the simple layout of the Cooper 500 racers, which had in turn borrowed their transverse-leaf-spring suspension layout from the Fiat Topolino. He even had a Cooper to copy from: he now rented a small workshop from a local garage owner, Vin Davison, and Vin (later of AC) looked after a racing Cooper for Eric Winterbottom.

Toj's second-hand car business had taught him to be a welder and after a fair amount of trial and error, he eventually gas-welded a frame that he was happy with, and the rest of that story, via Vin Davison, Cliff Davis and Ernie Bailey, is the story of how AC came to build the Ace. He says now that of the two dozen or so cars he built, LOY 500 (Cliff Davis's ultra-successful Bristol-engined car and the one that first caught the eyes of the Hurlock brothers), is still the one that he remembers with the greatest affection.

Through the early, Ace-type ladder frames, Tojeiro made a lot of racing contacts, and gained a reputation as a very successful racing chassis builder, even though he had done no more than a handful of cars before his AC contacts.

After that, his chassis became more elaborate, and even more successful. He started to build spaceframes, with proper wishbone suspension, freely admitting that the transverse leaf had been something of a stopgap. His first spaceframe was given the Lea Francis engine that had come out of Vin Davison's Tojeiro chassis, the one that became the prototype Ace. And it was driven by Cliff Davis whose LOY 500 and JOY 500 cars inspired the Ace's bodywork. It was a small world in those days.

The next chassis, in 1956, was for a Jaguar-engined car for John Ogier, and it was one of the lightest and quickest of all the many Jaguar-engined sports cars around at the time – lighter even than the monocoque D-Type. Late in 1956, John Bolster of *Autosport* tested it and reported that it was the quickest car he had tested to date, with a top speed of over 152mph (244kph) and 0–100mph (161kph) in 12.6 seconds. World champions Jack Brabham, Graham Hill and Jim Clark were among the many people who drove Tojeiros on occasion.

Toj's business was now big enough for him to be machining parts himself that he had previously had to buy in, and this precision engineering side of the set-up began to supply parts to other people. He even built a rolling chassis with a Coventry-Climax 1,100 engine for one Major Hope of the US Air

Force, as the basis for a proposed sports car, but although one chassis was eventually delivered, nothing else came of it.

Alongside the highly successful Jaguar-engined cars, he built a few smaller-engined ones, too, but not with the same sucess, and his last chassis was a small mid-engined sports car for Ecurie Ecosse in 1962. After that, he concentrated on the engineering side of the business until 1970 when he bought a well-established plastic moulding company, which he ran until the early 1980s.

John Tojeiro still has a Cobra connection in that he is now engineering director for DJ Sportscars, one of the better 'replica' makers, with the Dax, and he will be celebrating his forty years of involvement in motor racing with a special run of five Jaguar-engined cars, one replica of each of his most successful chassis.

They will be hand-built to the original specifications, bodied by doyen of racing body builders Maurice Gomm, and will have engines prepared in consultation with ex-Ecurie Ecosse Jaguar tuning wizard Wilkie Wilkinson.

At £250,000 per car, they represent a slightly better proposition for Toj than the £500 total royalty he earned from the Ace.

For Le Mans 1958, John Tojeiro built this streamlined Bristol-engined racer
for AC around a full spaceframe chassis with coil-spring suspension all round.
It finished eighth, but the production Ace stuck with its leaf springs.

into the car for AC's 1953 Earls Court Show stand, and then turning the show car into a production car.

That would involve both mechanical and cosmetic surgery. Visually, in becoming the AC show car, the Davison-Tojeiro racer changed its cast-alloy wheels for the centre-lock, knock-off, chromed wire ones that roadgoing sports car enthusiasts still preferred, and which showed off the prototype's polished and drilled Alfin brake drums. It gained a flat but now framed glass windscreen in place of Davison's frameless curved Perspex affair, a fully-trimmed cockpit with split-bench seat, and a hood and sliding Perspex sidescreens, not dissimilar to the ones that would still be offered by the time the Cobra arrived. It was re-registered to AC as TPL 792.

The most predictable mechanical change was to fit the traditional AC six-cylinder engine – thirty-four years old even by 1953, but still well respected for its light weight and outstanding smoothness.

THE ACE ON SHOW

Alongside the Tojeiro Ace was a bare rolling chassis, numbered AE01 and registered UPJ 75, also with AC engine. This was the first Ace chassis to be built by AC themselves, with assorted modifications from the Tojeiro basics for its new production role.

Neither the complete car nor the bare chassis were in final production form – there had been nothing like enough time for that – but they were well on the way.

The chassis had been beefed up for roadgoing reliability with the same size main tubes but in a heavier gauge steel. There was a stronger front box-section crossmem-

The very first Ace exhibits at Earls Court in 1953. The hastily completed and not quite finalized car is in the background; the first AC-built chassis, AE01, is in the foreground.

Show chassis AE01 turned into the first 'production' Ace, UPJ 75, with subtly revised nose and tail treatments and, of course, Weller's six-cylinder AC engine.

ber, and a modified AC 2-litre saloon radiator. The radiator was ahead of the front suspension assembly, and the steering gear (which at this stage was still of rack-and-pinion type) was mounted on the back of the front suspension box-member.

The rear-axle assembly used an ENV hypoid-bevel differential, rigidly housed in the rear box-section and driving through short, heavy-duty shafts with Hardy Spicer type universal joints inboard and outboard. Inside the Alfin finned brake drums were Girling hydraulic brakes and the dampers were telescopic Armstrongs, top-mounted

directly onto the box-member at the front, and onto a high cross-tube at the rear. They were chromed on the highly finished and very attractive show chassis.

At this stage, the lower wishbones were simple tubular fabrications with no added bracing, just as on the original Tojeiro; later Aces gained reinforcing webs inside the wishbones. All the suspension uprights were fabricated units and the flat rectangular petrol tank was slung out behind the rear axle. The gearbox was a Moss four-speed unit, with no call for a remote change mechanism because the engine and gearbox

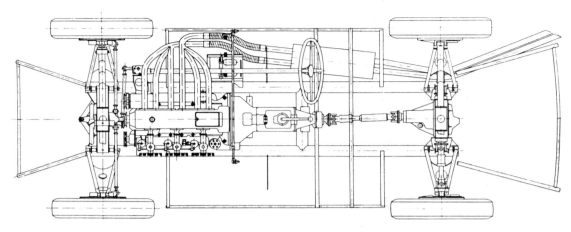

The basic layout of the AC-engined Ace chassis, with two massive main tubes, transverse leaf spring upper links with lower wishbones, and very little else. Aside from the engine, the layout looked little different in the leaf-spring Cobra.

assembly were mounted so far back in the chassis. That also meant that the car needed only a very short propshaft, with Hardy Spicer joints at each end, to the nose of the diff.

Even as it made its first appearance at that 1953 Show, the Ace prototype was very close indeed to the first-generation, transverse leaf-spring Cobra chassis of almost a decade later.

For production, the steering mechanism was changed from rack-and-pinion to worm-and-sector with a control arm to an idler arm behind the front box-member and links from the idler to the steering arms. That was largely to accommodate better the unavoidably large suspension geometry variations inherent in the simple transverse-leaf top-link layout, notably a tendency to create toe-in on compression with the original layout. It would last right through to the second series of Cobras, when the rack-and-pinion was finally made to work properly thanks to revised geometry.

Between the Tojeiro and the Ace, AC also improved the hubs and kingpins, adopted 16in (407mm) wire wheels with offset rims to improve straightline stability and, after starting with narrow-section cross-ply Dunlops on early cars, started fitting Michelin X tyres – a first for a genuine sports car. The radial Xs with their relatively soft sidewalls were chosen because they worked especially well with the marked geometry changes of the original suspension layout.

ARRIVING AT THE ACE SHAPE

The body changed too, initially around the nose, with the headlights being raised by some six inches in deference to US requirements because the Ace's main *raison d'être* was to be exported. That made room for sidelights below the headlamps and above the exaggerated forward droop of the bonnet styling line. The grille was toned down gently, slightly recessed and given a forward rather than a rearward slant.

The overall effect was to make the whole front end look shorter and chunkier than Tojeiro's original, and conveniently less Ferrari-like.

The ACE Two-seater Sports

The ACE Two-seater Sports

BEAUTIFUL body styling has been achieved by skilful design. The lightweight aluminium panelled body on steel tube framing provides great strength and durability, and reduces body weight to a minimum. Adequate all-weather protection is provided by hood and rigid Perspex sidescreens. Body trimming is in leather throughout.

THIS exciting car of character has the essential features required by the Sportsman. The ultra lightweight chassis provides a power weight ratio to allow exceptional acceleration and road speeds in excess of 100 miles per hour.

Subtle changes show up between the first renderings of the prototype Ace in an early brochure, and the actual production car. The headlamps are higher, the nose shorter and less droopy, and the tail is squarer. The first pictures show the ventilated Alfin brake drums of the show car, which did not make it from prototype to production. The robust simplicity of the chassis is obvious from this angle.

Technical Excellence

Designed by enthusiasts for enthusiasts. Independent suspension on all four wheels by transverse leaf springs and wishbones. Hand-built to a tight specification. Correct weight distribution. Ideal sought and attained.

The chassis illustration will be of interest, as it clearly shows the layout of the rear axle. It should, however, be pointed out that this is not the normal angle of drive, when loaded the halfshafts are practically level.

Tubular construction of the chassis and body framing provides tremendous strength, from the robust 3″ tubing of the main chassis frame to the 1¼″ scuttle anti roll bar and the ⅜″ body assembly tube, the whole welded to provide a simple yet robust structure.

The full flow exhaust manifolds will be observed, two branches of three pipes finally merge into two, proceeding through the silencer in dual form and continuing to atmosphere. The weight distribution is such that there is 18% more on the rear wheels than on the front. This is another feature which has assisted in providing the stability for which this Ace chassis is now well renowned. Centre lock wire wheels and Al-Fin brakedrums are included in the standard specification.

The Aceca specification from the chassis point of view differs only in the final axle ratio, and the fact that the differential is rubber mounted.

The all weather equipment can be viewed in this illustration. Use is made of plastic hooding which has the advantages of remaining impervious to the sun, and is also easily cleaned, the whole being stretched over two steel detachable uprights. Rigid perspex sidescreens 3/16″ thick provide their own support, and the rear portion swivels forward from a fulcrum in the centre middle corner. This produces an easy means of entry, and also allows simple and unobstructed hand signalling.

The overriders on view in the front are optional extras.

It also, unfortunately, spoiled the nice visual balance between the front and the original steeply raked tail, so that was modified too. AC gave the rump a taller, squarer profile, which restored the proportions and fortuitously gave the production Ace a lot more boot space than the Tojeiro-based prototype had had.

It was, and is, an outstandingly beautiful shape. AC kept it as simple as possible, with nothing more than vertical overriders front and back but no bumpers in the conventional sense – except for the US market, for which unattractive tubular bars were fitted in addition to the overriders. The rear lights were just small round lenses, there were no external door handles, and virtually the only break in the extraordinarily clean line was the flip-up fuel-filler cap on top of the left rear wing.

The shape as launched was the definitive Ace shape. It changed very little at all through the life of the Ace, changed only marginally for the 'small' Cobra, and is still instantly recognizable in pumped-up form in the more muscular 427.

The modifications were made during the winter of 1953–54, and the Ace went on sale during May 1954, starting from chassis number AE22. AE stood for AC engine; subsequently, AEX denoted an AC engine and left-hand drive, and the X-suffix then always referred to export cars; BE meant a Bristol engine; and RS was for the later cars with Rudd-tuned Ford engines.

When the prototype Ace was first shown in 1953, the quoted output for the standard AC 2-litre six-cylinder in other applications (to wit, the 2-litre saloon and Buckland tourer) was 75bhp, on three SU carbs and a 6.5:1 compression ratio, or from 1951 85bhp on an optional 7.0:1 compression. In both cases, the redline was limited by piston speed in the long-stroke engine, to a modest 4,500rpm. The long stroke, however, made the peak torque a bit more impressive, at 105lb ft, right down at 2750rpm.

In the show cars, the UMR CR series engine was also said to produce 85bhp, mainly by virtue of a compression ratio raised to 7.5:1, with the torque peak unchanged, and that was how the engine went into production.

It may have sounded a modest power output, but that was where Toj's philosophy of building as light as possible came into the picture. The Ace had been kept as simple as possible and therefore as light as possible. There was no extraneous trim, just two comfortable leather-bound bucket seats and leather-thong inside door pulls. The top and side curtains, which carried over pretty well unchanged to the Cobra, were simply detachable to stow in the boot. There was nothing there that did not need to be there.

On that basis, the Ace weighed very little more than the racing Tojeiro: 1,685lb (764kg) according to AC, which even with only 85bhp gave the respectable power to weight ratio of 113bhp per ton – about the equivalent of a minor-league hot hatchback in today's terms.

100 PLUS – BUT ONLY JUST

Pushing the Ace along at 21.4mph (34.4kph) per 1,000rpm in top, maximum power revs (which coincided with the supposed redline) would not quite have seen the Ace to 100mph (161kph), but early testers were told that they could use 5,000rpm in small doses. On that basis, the best two-way maximum reported for an AC-engined Ace came from the first wholly AC car, UPJ 75, built up on the bare show chassis. That was tested by *Motor* magazine in 1954 at 103mph (166kph), with a 0–60 time of 11.4 seconds.

AC still had an eye to motor sport for improving the breed and the image. They entered the Tojeiro show car, TPL 792, in the 1953 RAC Rally for Cliff Davis and

This is a very late model Ace, but the uncluttered simplicity of the cockpit, even down to leather-thong door pulls, is little changed from the original.

David Blakeley, and used it extensively for development through the winter. That confirmed, in particular, that a bit more than the original 85bhp and 4,500rpm limit would be needed to guarantee a genuine 100mph top speed, without which it did not look nearly so attractive against the opposition. It was not cheap, either, at a price of £1,439 as launched, against only £1,064 for the Austin-Healey 100-4 (with very similar top speed) or £1,616 for the much quicker XK120 drophead coupe, which had proved it really could beat 120mph (193kph). What the Ace buyer *was* getting, though, was a delicacy of handling and a degree of individuality that the mass-produced cars, however good, just could not match.

The Ace was developed through competition as well as on the road, notably in

rallying, and at the 1954 Motor Show AC launched a beautiful-looking coupe based on the Ace, the Aceca. That was one variant that did not carry on into the Cobra era, but over the years a total of 349 Acecas were built, compared to 694 Aces.

The production run started slowly. Through the rest of 1954, AC built twenty-two Aces, plus one Ace that was turned into the first Aceca. It continued to sell in growing numbers for the next three years: sixty-two in 1955, 110 in 1956 and 176 in 1957, which was the most it ever reached in a single year, even though it stayed in production until 1964. In all, AC built some 260 AC-engined Aces, 466 Bristol-engined ones and just thirty-seven with the Ford engine – less than 800 cars in total over a period of ten years. Not surprisingly, perhaps, given such

The original prototype, re-registered TPL 792, worked hard for its living after the launch, as both a rally car . . .

. . . and as a racer, driven here by the original owner, Vin Davison, at Silverstone in 1954.

In 1954, AC referred to it as the 'Ace Coupe', but when it went into production it became the Aceca.

tiny numbers, despite the car's success in small-volume manufacturer terms, AC made no profits from car manufacturing during the Ace period. They did, however, remain profitable overall thanks to outside contracts such as those for invalid cars and aero industry parts.

THE POWER STRUGGLE

Throughout the life of the Ace, AC did what they could to squeeze more power out of the old six-cylinder engine, but they were fundamentally hampered by its inability to rev safely beyond an occasional 5,000rpm, mainly limited by the valve gear. In 1955, however, the CL series engine (with improved bearings and lubrication, and with compression raised to 8.0:1), took the quoted output to 90bhp at 4,500rpm and 110lb ft of torque at only 2,500rpm.

The final power lift for the AC engine for the Ace came with the CLB series in 1958, when compression went up to 9.0:1, power to 102bhp at the previously forbidden crankshaft speed of 5,000rpm. A nitrided crankshaft on the later CLBN series engines made those revs rather safer, but it was clear that this was as far as the old engine could reliably go in production form, and although the final AC-engined Aces were not built until into the 1960s (which meant the engine had been produced during six decades), AC had had a splendid alternative since 1956.

That was the six-cylinder Bristol engine, which had more or less the same capacity as the AC engine (at 1,971cc, compared to 1,991cc) but was capable of producing a great deal more power, and doing so very reliably.

Like the AC engine, it wasn't exactly in its first flush of youth, dating back to a BMW design of 1936, but it had effectively been reborn after World War II when the design had been acquired by Bristol and substantially revamped, especially in so far as having much improved metallurgy and build quality.

Its bore to stroke relationship was barely any better than the old long-stroke AC six's, but with its brilliantly effective valvegear it scored heavily over the AC unit in its ability to rev freely without breaking. Where the AC engine had an aluminium alloy block and cast-iron head, the Bristol had an iron block and alloy head. Where the AC engine had reached its production peak at 102bhp, the Bristol engine had proved good for as much as 150bhp in racing form. Even the standard production versions in the Bristol 404 were offering from 105 to 125bhp at 4,500rpm, depending on spec, by the mid-1950s.

THE ACE BRISTOL

THE Ace's brilliant handling and the Bristol six's reliable power were first brought together early in 1956, not by AC themselves but by racing driver and AC dealer Ken Rudd.

Rudd, who had a garage at Worthing on the south coast, had done very well with his 1954 AC-powered Ace, VPL 422, but more by virtue of its chassis than its power, even when wrung right out to a reliable 105bhp. At the 1956 Easter Goodwood meeting, he appeared with a race-tuned version of the Bristol engine in his Ace and won the production sports car race. By the end of the year he had won the *Autosport* production sports car Championship.

AC were quick to spot the potential of the Bristol engine for the production Ace, with the only real drawback being that it would be substantially more expensive than the homegrown AC engine, which was already expensive enough compared to real mass-produced engines. On that basis, they began to offer the Bristol engine as an option,

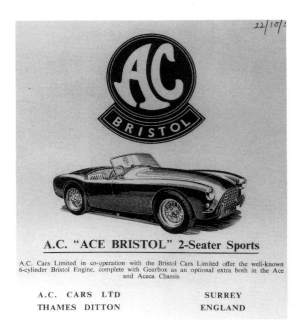

A.C. "ACE BRISTOL" 2-Seater Sports

A.C. Cars Limited in co-operation with the Bristol Cars Limited offer the well-known 6-cylinder Bristol Engine, complete with Gearbox as an optional extra both in the Ace and Aceca Chassis

| A.C. CARS LTD | SURREY |
| THAMES DITTON | ENGLAND |

Bristol power gave the Ace a new lease of life from 1956, prompted by AC dealer Ken Rudd's successful racing conversion in his own Ace. The Ace Bristol sold far more than any other Ace, right up to 1963.

primarily for competition, and launched the Ace-Bristol at the 1956 Earls Court Motor Show alongside a Bristol version of the Aceca coupe. Soon, AC were using more Bristol engines than Bristol themselves, and eventually built some 465 Bristol-powered Aces between 1956 and 1963, plus 170 Aceca-Bristols.

They offered the engine initially in what Bristol designated 100B tune. That meant 105bhp at 5,000rpm on an 8.5:1 compression ratio and three downdraught Solex carburettors. AC used the engine in conjunction with Bristol's own close-ratio four-speed gearbox in place of the usual Moss box that came with the AC-engined car, and added Laycock overdrive, which operated on the top three gears. In later years, Bristol owners who preferred AC's modification for

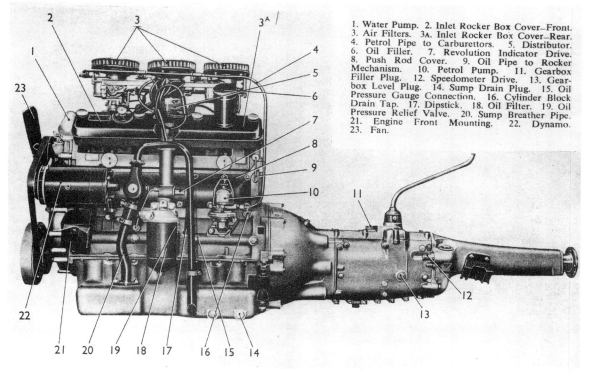

1. Water Pump. 2. Inlet Rocker Box Cover–Front.
3. Air Filters. 3ᴀ. Inlet Rocker Box Cover–Rear.
4. Petrol Pipe to Carburettors. 5. Distributor.
6. Oil Filler. 7. Revolution Indicator Drive.
8. Push Rod Cover. 9. Oil Pipe to Rocker
Mechanism. 10. Petrol Pump. 11. Gearbox
Filler Plug. 12. Speedometer Drive. 13. Gearbox Level Plug. 14. Sump Drain Plug. 15. Oil
Pressure Gauge Connection. 16. Cylinder Block
Drain Tap. 17. Dipstick. 18. Oil Filter. 19. Oil
Pressure Relief Valve. 20. Sump Breather Pipe.
21. Engine Front Mounting. 22. Dynamo.
23. Fan.

THE BRISTOL 100D2 ENGINE (nearside)

The Bristol engine was based on Fritz Fiedler's pre-war BMW six-cylinder design, acquired by Bristol as war reparations and considerably improved upon. Inclined valves in hemispherical combustion chambers were worked by a single side cam via ingenious crossover pushrods.

the Ace of a fixed first gear instead of the Bristol 'freewheel' type, formed a queue at AC's stores. In 1961, after the Bristol engine went out of production at Filton, they were queuing at Thames Ditton for 100D2 engines, too.

The D2 was the highest spec Bristol engine offered by AC for the Ace. The 100D engine, unique to AC, was introduced in 1957, and virtually all the Aces sold that year used it in preference to the milder 100B. The 100D gave 120bhp at 5,750rpm. The 100D2, as used by Rudd in 170 DPC at Le Mans in 1957, was introduced in the production Ace for 1958. With a 9.0:1 compression ratio, modified Solex carburettors and a 'big nose' crankshaft with Holset viscous damper, it gave 128bhp at 5,750rpm.

At Le Mans, Rudd's D2-engined Ace, with cowled air intake, partly faired undertray, small windscreen and virtually no trim, managed almost 130mph (209kph) on the Mulsanne straight, lapped at over 100mph (161kph) and averaged 97mph (156kph) for the twenty-four hours.

Even for the road, the Ace-Bristol was a good deal quicker than the standard Ace, with a top speed of as much as 117mph (188kph) and 0–60mph (96.5kph) in under ten seconds even in standard production trim. From 1957 it also offered the option of front disc brakes, as first tried on Rudd's 1957 Le Mans car. From 1959 there was a new gearbox option with TR2 gears in a lightweight AC case, and a short remote change instead of the original cranked lever.

RACING SUCCESSES

The Ace-Bristol quickly made a name for itself in racing, both in Europe and in the USA, from club level to Le Mans and especially in the SCCA Production Championships. There, Ace-Bristols won Class E in 1957, 1958 and 1959; the authorities moved them into Class D for 1960 but they won there, too; and in 1961 when they were obliged to move up to Class C (as previously won by Mercedes, Ferrari, and Porsche), they won again.

Among the interested parties watching the SCCA domination would have been Carroll Shelby, nearing the end of his racing career and starting to think about his sports car project. And in 1959, the year when Shelby won Le Mans for Aston Martin, a near-standard Ace-Bristol entered by Rudd, driven to and from the circuit and driven in the race by Jack Turner and Ted Whiteaway, outlasted far faster opposition in a race decimated by heat, to win the 2-litre class and finish a creditable seventh overall.

The Ace was now moving into its final phase, and towards the hiatus in engine supply that would open the door for Shelby, Ford and AC to co-operate on turning the Ace into the Cobra.

FROM BRISTOL TO FORD

There was one more stage for the Ace before that happened, with a six-cylinder British Ford engine. Again, Rudd was the instigator.

The incentive to find another new engine was provided by struggling Bristol announcing in 1961 that they were about to switch to off-the-shelf Chrysler V8 power for their

An Ace Bristol in its element, drifting through one of Silverstone's high-speed curves, demonstrating the wonderful chassis balance that often made it quicker than far more powerful cars.

new 407, which meant the end of their six-cylinder production. In fact AC would be able to continue with existing Bristol engine stocks right up to 1963 (which only meant very small numbers by that stage) and they were even able to sell off around 100 engines from stock when they finally stopped using them in production.

This time, Rudd's alternative was less exotic than the complex BMW-based Bristol, but bigger, cheaper, easily tuned and capable of giving ample power. On the down side, it did not have anything like the thoroughbred character of either the Bristol or the old AC engine, but then even they had gradually lost much of their refinement as they had searched for more power.

The new engine was the 2.6-litre, pushrod overhead-valve, straight-six Ford Zephyr unit. Unlike either AC or Bristol engines, it was a modern 'oversquare' design with bigger bore than stroke, giving it the advantages of larger piston and valve areas and a more reliable ability to rev. Being all-iron it was heavier than either of its part-alloy Ace predecessors, so AC added an extra leaf to the front transverse spring, but it was lower than either of the old engines, which allowed a smoother restyling of the bonnet area, with a handsomely smaller grille.

Standard output in the Zephyr was only 85bhp, but it was a very tuneable engine. Under his Ruddspeed banner, Ken Rudd offered several stages of tune, with up to 170bhp to order. AC tested a 155bhp version in an Ace around March 1961 and decided almost immediately to adopt the engine for production, which had started by mid-1961.

Rudd's Stage 1 modifications had a modified cylinder head with big valves, and three 1.75-inch SU carburettors. Stage 2 was as Stage 1 but with lightweight pistons. Stage 3 used a light-alloy six-port Raymond Mays head, lightweight pistons and three SUs. Stage 4 was as Stage 3 but with three twin-choke Weber DCOE carburettors. These options gave 90, 125, 150 and 170bhp respectively. AC also threw away the standard Ford three-speed gearbox and mated the Zephyr engine to their own gearbox. Front disc brakes became standard.

The Ace 2.6, even in Stage 5 tune, was considerably cheaper than the Bristol-engined car that continued alongside it (though still more expensive than most of the mainstream opposition), and in its higher stages of tune it was markedly faster and more flexible than the Ace-Bristol.

Unfortunately, the Ford engine had its faults, notably with the bottom end, which became more and more prone to failure as the power went up – especially if owners chose to ignore Ruddspeed's carefully calculated rev limits. Ford did produce a much improved version in 1962 for the Zephyr MkIV, with stronger crank and better bearings, but they were too late for all but one or two Ace 2.6s.

In all, only thirty-seven Ford-engined Aces and just eight Acecas were built, which was a clear enough sign that the Ace had reached the end of the road.

But not quite, because in September 1961, just as the supplies of Bristol engines were drying up and even before the Ford 2.6 had got into its stride, a letter arrived on Charles Hurlock's desk from Carroll Shelby, with an outline idea for putting a US V8 engine into the Ace and creating a rather special kind of sports car.

4 Developing the Cobra

By 1961, Bristol had decided to stop producing their six-cylinder engine and Carroll Shelby was no longer a racing driver.

Bristol had solved their problems of lack of power and too much cost by dropping the faithful old BMW-based six and adopting an off-the-shelf Chrysler V8 engine with Torqueflite auto transmission for their next model, the 407.

Shelby was in California trying to bring together the basic elements of an Anglo-American sports car to beat the world. In creating their hybrid, Bristol finally allowed Shelby to produce his. In the middle were AC Cars with their Ace sports car, and the Ford Motor Co with a new, lightweight engine. Shelby put the whole jigsaw together and came up with the Cobra.

In 1959, he had reached the pinnacle of his racing career (to the outside world, at least) with his Le Mans win for Aston Martin. He had gone back to Europe in the late 1950s to race, but he admits now that he also went back to pick up as many tips as he could on building European style sports cars, and especially to make the right sort of contacts.

He was reluctantly starting to accept that his racing career would not last much longer. Even as a successful sports car racer, he was not exactly getting rich. Then, during 1960, he had started to have the recurrence of his childhood chest pains that were eventually diagnosed as his heart problem.

In February 1960 he had moved to California, largely to be close to the racing community – not because he planned to continue racing long term but, again, because of the car building talent that lived in that area.

He was trying to do a lot of things at the same time. For the moment, he was still racing; he was opening his racing drivers' school; he was running his Goodyear racing-tyre dealership; he had a heart problem; and he was mid-way through a divorce brought on by all the other things he was trying to cope with.

And on top of all of them, he had his increasingly consuming plan to build a sports car. It would be a European-style sports car with American power. It would be meant for the road, of course, but maybe only with an eye on getting the numbers up for homologation and, in the longer term, it probably already included that motivating desire to whip Enzo Ferrari's ass.

PUTTING OUT FEELERS

As long ago as 1957, he had discussed the sports-car idea several times with personal contacts at General Motors, notably with Ed Cole, who was Chevrolet's chief engineer, and Harley Earl, vice president of styling.

Shelby's thoughts at that early stage had revolved around taking a Corvette chassis and running gear and paring it down with a lighter body and more basic equipment. With its glassfibre shell and separate chassis (as opposed to the increasingly common unit-construction) the Corvette would have lent itself well to the change. Cole and Earl both saw possibilities in the scheme, but General Motors's management did not.

They may have been more than usually cautious because they had only started to make the Corvette itself a sales success in the past few months. It had been a disaster as launched, with good looks and a good

*Planning his sports car, Shelby looked at the Corvette as a base but did not like
GM bureaucracy. By 1960, the Corvette had overcome initial mediocrity and
was a huge success. It was always the Cobra's main opposition. This is one of
Briggs Cunningham's 1960 Le Mans entries, driven to eighth place by Jon Fitch
and Bob Grossman.*

chassis, completely thrown away by a miser-
ably inadequate six-cylinder engine and
automatic transmission. In fact, the Corvette's early problems were far worse even than
the Ace's problems with its ageing AC six.

General Motors (GM) finally gave the
Corvette a V8 for 1955, refined the suspension geometry and restyled it for 1956, at the
same time giving it a lot more of the
performance it always looked as though it
had. It still had a problem in being more
expensive than Ford's big-selling new Thunderbird, and a bit too expensive for the
young market it should really have hit, but
at least now they were starting to sell
reasonable numbers. Shelby's idea might
have given GM a car to sell below the
Corvette but, having lost out so badly with
it thus far, probably the last thing they
needed now that it was starting to sell was
to create their own competitor.

In any case, Shelby had seen the worst
side of big-league corporate management in
GM, where the wheels did grind exceedingly
slowly, and it was not really the sort of
relationship he had had in mind; he just
wanted to get things done. So when Shelby
arrived in California he still had no more
than a vague idea of how his car was going
to happen, save that it would have a so far
indeterminate V8 engine in an equally
indeterminate European-style chassis. Having drawn a blank on the Corvette, he would
have liked a Healey-type chassis, but prefer-
ably a tubular one for adaptability.

As well as talking to GM, Shelby had
already approached several European car
makers with outline proposals, but without
so much as a firm idea of what he would be
offering as an engine. He was not naive, just
keen to get things moving, and he could let
the details wait until later.

A RACER NO MORE

The project became slightly more feasible after 4 December 1960, when Shelby, in a T61 'Birdcage' Maserati, finished fifth in the third Annual Times Mirror Grand Prix for Sports Cars at Riverside. It was his last race; between the heart problems and everything else, it was time to call it a day.

His racing school was his answer to getting out of being a racing driver. It would let him be involved with racing and, especially, it would let him stay in touch with racing people, without the stress and the commitment of competing. The school started with a $90 advertisement in the motoring press, which brought a $1,400 response – 1,400 requests for more information, at a dollar each. On the strength of that, the Shelby School of High Performance Driving was up and running by 1961, based on the Riverside circuit.

Shelby had moved from his first Califor-nian base of La Mirada, a small town near Disneyland in the south-east Los Angeles area, to Santa Fe Springs. Aside from a secretary/telephonist, his first employee was Peter Brock, who was only twenty-three years old in 1961 but who had already spent a year with General Motors, where he had been involved in styling the new Sting Ray. He left because, like Shelby, he could not cope with the big corporation's slowness in making decisions. Brock was an amateur racing driver himself, too, latterly running a Lotus 19.

The school was as successful as the response had suggested. Shelby worked on the basis of renting track time week by week at favourable rates, for once minimizing his investment risk. It was real income, too; the school provided virtually individual tuition for maybe a week at a time – depending on ability to learn – either in the pupil's own car or in one provided by the school, for a fee, of course.

The Corvette Stingray, in which Pete Brock had been briefly involved, was a very different style of Corvette, but still the car that Cobra had to beat.

The big Healey (with a bigger bonnet perhaps) was another obvious possibility for Shelby's ideas, but BMC management were happy with the car as it was.

Brock was involved with the school from the very beginning, mainly as a teacher, but also as an engineer for ongoing projects and as a capable administrator. Later, he designed all the Cobra graphics, did many of the early press ads, raced, ran the school and also organized Shelby's accessories business. And he designed the Daytona coupe. He was just what Shelby needed at the time, someone he trusted to take most of the workload while he concentrated on his business commitments and his sports car plans.

Fundamentally, those plans now revolved around building at least 100 cars – the magic number for homologation – with the majority to be sold as road cars to finance the ones that would remain as racers. Shelby had no facilities (nor finance) to build that number of chassis himself, so he was looking for an outside source.

He needed a strong chassis to take the weight and torque of a powerful V8, and a wide chasis to accommodate the V8 engine configuration. Even while he was still racing, he had spoken to Aston Martin, De Tomaso, Maserati and to Jensen. He had asked his friend Donald Healey to supply Healey chassis on which to base his car, and Healey might have happily obliged but his new benefactors at Austin would not let him.

THE PIECES COME TOGETHER

Then, in 1961, Shelby heard from a journalist friend, John Christy at *Sports Car Graphic* magazine, that AC Cars were just about to lose the supply of Bristol engines that had made their little Ace such a difficult package to beat in SCCA racing and elsewhere for so many recent years. Shelby borrowed an Ace-Bristol to have a better look and immediately saw the potential.

Wasting no time, he telephoned AC and spoke to works director Harry Sidney, who confirmed that the situation was indeed as Shelby had heard and that the Bristol engine really was about to be lost to AC.

Shelby may also have learned that AC had been looking for some time at whatever other possibilities might be available as a replacement – not only at the in-line six-cylinder Ford 2.6 Zephyr engine that they did briefly adopt, but also at engines as diverse as the inevitable six-cylinder Jaguar, the V8 Daimler, and the all-aluminium US Buick V8.

AC had not actually tried it themselves, but a couple of US racers, inevitably, had already put V8 engines into Ace chassis. As early as 1957, an east-coast racer by the name of Roger Wing had put a Chevy V8 into his Ace-Bristol and had a reasonable amount of racing success with it; and Jerry Scheberies, helped by Walt Petersen, later put an F85 Oldsmobile engine (aka the light-alloy Buick V8, later Rover V8) into his 1958 Ace, mated to a Corvette transmission. That was after the Cobra, and Scheberies called his car the Mongoose – after all, a mongoose kills snakes.

Back in Britain, sixes were more common than V8s. The excellent Jaguar six had been tried in the Ace chassis by several customers, but in reality it was too big and too heavy to retain the Ace's all-important handling edge. The lightweight if frequently fragile Daimler V8 was ruled out politically because Daimler's own SP250 Dart sports car competed as directly as anything against the Ace in the production sports car market. Rudd had favoured the light-alloy Buick V8, and AC could see its potential, but at that point the engine was still in production at GM and very expensive. Buying in supplies would have been a different proposition from what Rover did a few years later in buying the manufacturing rights.

So, AC were interested to listen to Shelby's ideas, vague as they were, on the basis of opening up the possibilities. Shelby sent his airmail letter to Charles Hurlock on 8 September 1961. He had not got a definite engine plan at the time, but he had thought about either a small-block Chevy, or the familiar Buick alloy V8. His faith in General Motors, however, was strictly limited by his earlier approaches.

THE FORD CONNECTION

Without knowing it, though, Shelby had already made the contact that turned the whole project into a serious possibility. On 4 July 1961, engineer Dave Evans had been at the Pikes Peak hillclimb, representing Ford, and Shelby had been there on behalf of Goodyear. At the time, Evans was in charge of Ford's NASCAR stock-car racing programme, and especially involved with the engine development side.

This was a time of change for Ford. In 1960 they produced just a couple of modestly high-performance cars and had long been surviving on an image of steadiness and safety consciousness. Within a couple of years, Ford had tried to buy Ferrari, failed, and started a racing division of their own: Ford Advanced Vehicles. Within a couple more years, they had won Le Mans for the first time with the GT40 and a lot of help from Shelby, and they had established the philosophy of 'Total Performance'.

That was Ford on the world motor racing scene, as masterminded by Lee Iacocca, head of the Ford Division of Ford Motor Co since 1960, and it is fundamental to the timing of the Cobra story.

Total Performance was great for racing, but it was not just for glory itself; glory sells cars and that is what Ford are in business to do. Iacocca's basic premise was that Ford needed to improve their image, to make it more sophisticated. Iacocca, son of Italian

Ford's NASCAR cars were a very different proposition from the small, lithe Cobra, but the NASCAR programme provided the basic motor sport contacts. This is Bob Conner in trouble with a 427cu in stocker.

immigrant parents and a car enthusiast through and through (which is not always a top motor executive credential), loved European sports cars and European racing. Anything that gave Ford in the US showroom a tinge of European glamour was deemed to be good.

Meanwhile, the domestic racing scene was what America watched, and for a huge majority of American enthusiasts, that did not mean European-style road racing; it meant US-style oval track racing, and especially the big NASCAR (and AAA) 'late model' stock cars.

In the early 1950s, American manufacturers had been happy to go racing under the new NASCAR banner in cars that bore at least a passing resemblance to showroom stock models. In 1954, NASCAR rules were re-written to say that stock cars must henceforth be truly stock, and not stock-plus options. The Big Three manufacturers, having been beaten by upstart Hudson for most of the early 1950s, were into NASCAR in a

big way, officially or unofficially; the 1954 'stock' ruling meant that the most powerful car a manufacturer could list as a stock model would henceforth be the most powerful car they could enter. The horsepower race was under way.

In 1954, with a new overhead-valve V8 for their Lincoln Capri, Ford officially returned to racing for the first time since the mid-1930s, via the Carrera Panamericana road race. Fords also became the cars to beat in NASCAR, though not factory cars because the factory refused to support racing directly. They were not averse to supplying special parts to dealers through the back door, of course, while having a strong anti-racing lobby up front.

It was largely because of Ford that in 1957 the Automobile Manufacturers' Association (AMA) 'recommended' that none of its members should participate in motor racing any more; which makes it ironic that in 1962 Henry Ford II was first among the big manufacturers to announce that they would

Henry Ford II (centre) set Ford back on the path to an official racing programme in 1962, and gave Iacocca the freedom to develop Total Performance.

no longer abide by the AMA's ruling on racing and that they were back in the game officially.

That was the background against which Shelby met Dave Evans at Pikes Peak. He did not specifically mention his sports car plans during that brief encounter and he had not even spoken to Evans again before he sent his letter to AC in September 1961. It was Ray Brock, editor of *Hot Rod* magazine, who put Shelby back in touch with Evans around October 1961. Brock had heard about Shelby's approach to AC and had also heard about an interesting new engine from Ford.

THE NEW FORD V8

The engine was all new, a lightweight cast-iron unit using new thin-wall casting techniques with extensive use of resin-bonded casting cores, to bring the weight down close to that of an alloy unit like the GM (later Rover) V8, but without the prohibitive costs. Cast iron with a high graphite content has very good lubrication properties and therefore good resistance to wear. It also had advantages in being both stiffer and quieter than an alloy unit, with fewer vibration damping problems and fewer thermal expansion problems.

As the Challenger 221 V8, the project dated back to 1958. It was started under the direction of Ford engineer Robert F. Stirrat as an engine for future Ford cars and even small trucks. It was launched in the 1961 Ford Fairlane, a new mid-sized car set between the compact Falcons and the big Galaxies.

The new V8 was offered in two versions: the 221cu in was the smallest V8 Ford had ever produced and also had the shortest stroke of any engine in its class, with a short, stiff, five-bearing crankshaft, which gave plenty of potential for high revs and for future tuning. In 221cu in form, with 3.5 × 2.875in bore and stroke (88.8 × 73.0mm and

POWER
TEAMS

OVERDRIVE

FAIRLANE OVERDRIVE (available with V-8 only). Automatic planetary-type fourth gear lets engine loaf along at fewer rpm's, saving gas all the time it's operating. You get more miles per gallon, longer engine life and this bonus: flooring the accelerator gives you instant downshift for passing. Overdrive is engaged and disengaged by single, simple control (illustrated).

FAIRLANE V-8

All new from carburetor to crankshaft! Ford-pioneered foundry techniques give this new V-8 the strength and durability of cast iron with the advantages of lighter weight metals. Result: more *working* horsepower per pound. Add in big-bore displacement (221 cu. in.) and super-short stroke (bore x stroke 3.50 x 2.87), and you have the remarkable combination of trigger-quick reflexes on a *regular* gas "diet." *Horsepower:* 145 at 4,400 rpm; *torque:* 216 lbs-ft at 2,200 rpm. Shown with Fordomatic Drive.

The new thinwall V8 was a major achievement for Ford, a cheap-to-make cast iron engine weighing little more than an exotic all-alloy unit. The 221 was the start of one of the finest engine ranges that Ford ever made, and ideal for Shelby.

3,621cc), it produced 145bhp at 4,400rpm on an 8.7:1 compression ratio.

Weighing in at around 450lb (204kg) bare, or 490lb (222kg) including all ancillaries, the ultra-compact engine was almost 200lb (90.5kg) lighter than the old 'Y-block' Ford V8s, and very little heavier than the six-cylinder Bristol engine in the Ace.

By the time the Fairlane was launched, there was also a 260cu in (4,260cc) version, with the same stroke but with bore enlarged to 3.8in (96.5mm), retaining the 8.7:1 compression ratio and running on a two-barrel Holley carburettor on a cast-iron manifold. That gave 164bhp at 4,400rpm and an impressive 258lb ft of torque, which was always the area where the lazy but big-capacity US V8s scored over a smaller European engine of similar horsepower.

When Shelby got back in touch with

Evans by letter, he knew no details about the engine beyond the fact that it existed. Evans must have seen some promise in Shelby's ideas because as soon as he had read the letter he phoned Shelby from Dearborn, to say that he was sending two engines for him to take a look at.

Evans was already working on the 260 version for competition, notably for the 1963 Falcon Sprint, in which Ford saw a possible answer to the success of the Chevy Monza. In fact one of the very first manifestations of Total Performance was a Falcon Sprint prepared in Britain by Alan Mann Racing, for the Monte Carlo Rally, where it did a lot better than most people expected. For the moment, though, Evans sent Shelby two basic 221s, without mentioning the 260.

By the time the two engines arrived in the Santa Fe Springs workshop that Shelby

When Ford launched the new lightweight, small-block V8 in the Fairlane, they began a shift in emphasis from conformity to performance.

shared with commercial tuning equipment specialist and drag racer Dean Moon, he had already sent another letter off to the Hurlocks at AC telling them of his progress. He also sent some basic weights and dimensions, suggested some chassis modifications that they could be putting in hand pending receipt of an engine, and asked them to think of any others they thought appropriate. That was in November 1961.

AN ENGINE TO THAMES DITTON

Shelby and Moon started to play with one of the engines, quickly coming to the conclusion that it was both rugged and highly tunable. Shelby air-freighted the other, complete with four-speed gearbox, to AC. When the crate arrived at AC, more or less unannounced, the storeman who first saw it read the Ford logo 'FoMoCo' stencilled on the crate and told his boss that it appeared that something had been sent from Japan.

All AC's drawings for the Cobra prototype had references to 'AC 3.6', consistent with the 3,621cc equivalent of the original 221cu in engine, but they may not have been sent what they thought. They never had cause to look inside the engine itself (which would have been outwardly identical to a 260) and when, after many years of sitting unused in the works, it was bought by AC Owners' Club stalwart Barrie Bird, it apparently proved to be a 260.

Vin Davison, owner of the original Tojeiro Ace, was still at AC when the engine arrived, and he set to work, with chief engineering designer Alan Turner and engineer Desmond Stratton, to get it into the car. Shelby, meanwhile, had another message from Dave Evans to tell him about the 260cu in (4,260cc) development and to tell him that another couple of engines in that size were on their way. Shelby immediately conveyed this to the Hurlocks, and from this point on the deal was coming together in leaps and bounds – to the extent that Shelby even scraped together the time and the air fare to go to Thames Ditton and help to finalize some of the details on the prototype during the winter of 1961–62.

It is worth pausing here to think what Shelby had actually achieved in no more than about four months from his first letter to Charles Hurlock. Even without a specific engine to offer, he had persuaded the Hurlocks that his idea was sound; he had found his engine – and probably a far more suitable engine than he ever dreamed he would find; he had persuaded Ford to supply the first engines on credit; he had persuaded AC to do the same with a chassis; and he had actually got engine and chassis into the same building.

He has always been generous with his credit to the other people involved, including the Hurlocks and their staff at AC, who, he reckons, were helpful and keen, even when the modifications proved to be more complicated than originally envisaged. And he has abundant praise for the people at Ford without whom he knows the Cobra would not have happened.

MANAGEMENT WITH IMAGINATION

Foremost amongst those people at Ford were Don Frey and Ray Geddes, management men who, at first glance, would hardly appear to be Shelby-type people, but who turned out to be exactly the hands-off type who Shelby could work with.

It was the ever-enthusiastic Dave Evans who put Shelby in touch with Frey. Frey was a Ford Division assistant general manager, a bespectacled, academic-looking type in his late thirties, but a genuinely knowledgable sports car enthusiast. He had even driven an Allard while he was in the army during the early 1950s. Very soon after the Shelby deal happened, Ford tried to buy out Ferrari as a short-cut into international racing, and Frey was one of the team sent to Maranello to

finalize the deal. He came very close but came up against the same Ferrari stubbornness that Shelby had already experienced.

Frey was definitely not the sort of corporate bean-counter who Shelby had developed such a dislike for in his earlier approaches to GM management. He was in charge of engineering planning in the Ford Division and liked quick decisions. After minimal consultation with higher powers at Ford, he gave Shelby an almost immediate go-ahead for his project and even suggested a line of credit for the first 100 engines from Ford! Shelby has described Frey as 'probably the most knowledgable racing executive in the world'.

Ford did want some financial control over the Shelby set-up, of course, but again Shelby struck lucky with someone he respected and who never made him feel stifled by bureaucracy. That was Ray Geddes, a young lawyer from the Ford financial office, with a master's degree in business management.

Ultimately, although Ford supplied both credit and financial management, they did not pay for the cars – Shelby did. And although Ford provided access to many other design, distribution and engineering facilities, they did not build the cars – AC and Shelby did.

INTO THE METAL

AC worked on the first prototype through the winter of 1961–62. As everyone had thought, there were few problems in fitting the V8 into the Ace's ample engine bay: it was less than 21in (535mm) long, only 16.5in (420mm) wide, and barely 15lb (6.5kg) heavier than a Bristol six. Fitting mainly meant devising new engine mounts and making sure that the exhaust system went in.

The four-speed Ford/Borg-Warner T10 gearbox was retained, for several reasons.

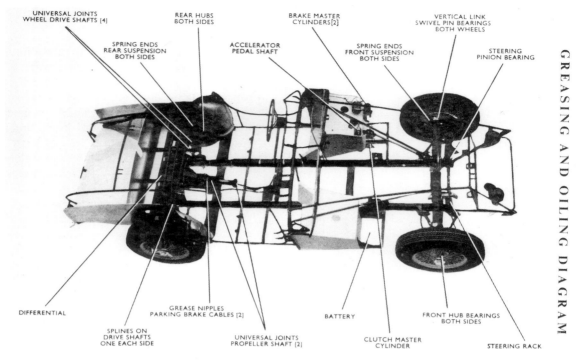

UNIVERSAL JOINTS
WHEEL DRIVE SHAFTS [4]

REAR HUBS
BOTH SIDES

BRAKE MASTER
CYLINDERS [2]

VERTICAL LINK
SWIVEL PIN BEARINGS
BOTH WHEELS

SPRING ENDS
REAR SUSPENSION
BOTH SIDES

ACCELERATOR
PEDAL SHAFT

SPRING ENDS
FRONT SUSPENSION
BOTH SIDES

STEERING
PINION BEARING

DIFFERENTIAL

GREASE NIPPLES
PARKING BRAKE CABLES [2]

BATTERY

FRONT HUB BEARINGS
BOTH SIDES

SPLINES ON
DRIVE SHAFTS
ONE EACH SIDE

UNIVERSAL JOINTS
PROPELLER SHAFT [2]

CLUTCH MASTER
CYLINDER

STEERING RACK

The simplicity of the leaf-spring Cobra chassis is evident in this maintenance diagram. The main chassis is no more than the two big tubes, the cross members and suspension carriers; the smaller lattice is the supporting frame for the Superleggera-type bodywork.

Obviously, it matched the engine directly without an adaptor plate; it was an all-syncromesh design; it was designed to take many times the torque limits of the old Bristol box; and it weighed only about 10lb (4.5kg) more than the existing unit. It was also easily obtainable – and that meant it was cheap.

That was the easy bit. A little more challenging was getting the Ace-type chassis to stay in one piece with around twice as much torque as it had ever been asked to handle before, or three times as much as it had been designed for in the first place, and the braking and cornering forces associated with a suddenly much quicker car.

Although John Tojeiro had built a space-framed, coil-sprung, streamlined car for AC for the 1958 Le Mans race, and could have done a similar chassis for the new car, Shelby's whole plot revolved around staying

with the simplicity of the ladder-framed, leaf-sprung Ace. So the first prototype chassis was basically identical to the Ace, with main tubes of the same diameter and the same 17in (430mm) distance apart, but in yet heavier gauge tubing.

In detail, though, it was unique in several ways. Most notably, it had inboard rear disc brakes with Girling calipers instead of the old outboard drums. That was presumably to reduce unsprung weight, but seems a strange move when you consider that the car was always intended for racing, where quick pad changes would be a major consideration. They may just have been taking advantage of existing mountings on the substantially beefed-up final-drive assembly, which was based around a Salisbury limited-slip diff derived from the Jaguar E-Type/MkX family. There were also heavier duty driveshafts and some additional bracing from the nose

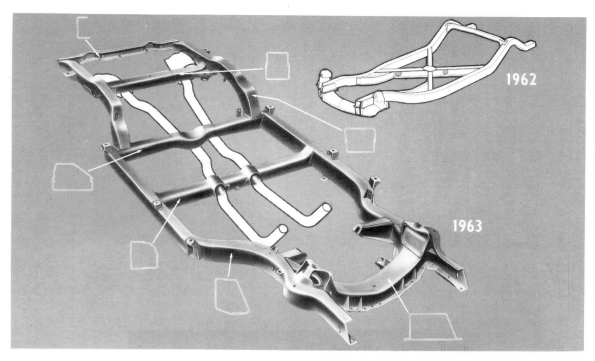

1962

1963

By contrast, the Corvette frame (as redesigned here for 1963, with wider side members to allow lower seating) was a conventional pressed-steel arrangement taking a bolt-on fibreglass shell.

of the diff to a new chassis cross-tube. A reinforcing frame of square-section tubes was added around the rear suspension mounts across the width of the car, and there were other additional bracing plates around the chassis, too.

Wheels from AC's Greyhound saloon were used, their bigger offset and slightly longer front transverse spring giving a small increase in track. Early testing, not on a finished car but on front-end components only, had shown that several items still tended to break when subjected to higher loads. Accordingly, the steering-box mounts, the hubs and the front kingpins were all upgraded.

THE PROTOTYPE RUNS

The first complete car ran for the first time in January 1962 at Silverstone, appropriately enough with Carroll Shelby driving, and

that was just *before* Ford had formally agreed to supply their engines in series.

After its brief British shakedown, the first prototype had the engine and gearbox removed (for customs purposes), and was airfreighted on 2 February 1962, via New York, to Los Angeles. It had chassis number CSX2000, the CSX standing for Carroll Shelby Experimental according to Shelby, or for Carroll Shelby Export according to AC.

While the car was in transit from Britain, it also gained a name: Cobra. Carroll Shelby says that the name came to him in a dream and he woke up and wrote it down on a pad. The nearest thing to a problem with using it was that it had been used as a trademark, in the 1940s, by American car-maker Crosley for their Copper-Brazed engines, but as Crosley had gone out of business in 1952, Ford and AC were happy to go ahead with it.

The full title of the car has never been quite so straightforward. AC always did want their name on the car in acknowledge-

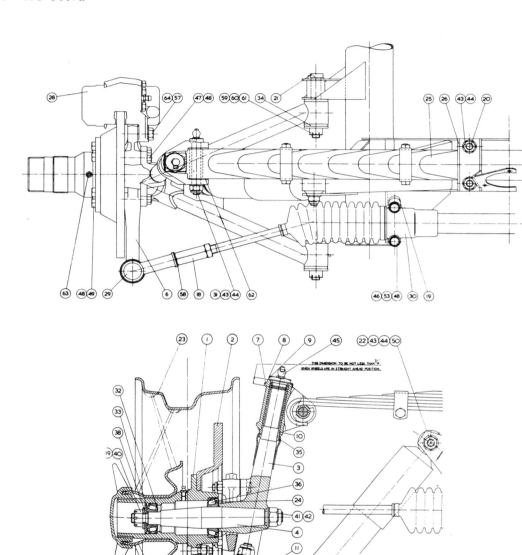

Cobra front suspension could hardly be simpler, with a single lower wishbone, and the transverse leaf providing both top link and springing medium. The assembly had been considerably upgraded from the Ace but was basically identical.

ment of their chassis; Ford originally *did not* want their name on the car but did insist on having Shelby's name on it. The very first car appeared as the Shelby Ford AC Cobra, but Ford's acknowledgement was soon replaced by discreet 'Powered by Ford' badges on the front flanks. So then the car was a Shelby AC/Cobra (strangely with the oblique between AC and Cobra as written in early ads); in Britain, where it would not go on sale for a long time yet anyway, it was normally just an AC Cobra (later, an AC 289 or an AC MkIV). Ford eventually came to own the Cobra name, leading to some late cars being known simply as Ford Cobras; they used the name later on Mustang-derived muscle-cars, and they have staunchly defended against its later misuse, particularly on 'replicas'.

THE FINAL STAGE

By any name, though, the Cobra had arrived. When CSX2000 landed at Los Angeles airport, Shelby had to borrow a trailer from a Ferrari-owning drivers' school pupil to go and collect it, towed by Dean Moon's truck. When it came out of the crate it was unpainted and covered with labels: 'For Export Only'; 'Add Oil Before Driving'; 'No water in the Engine'.

The last two labels were rather superfluous, as there was no engine in the car anyway. There was one in the workshop, though, and within eight hours of the car arriving at 10820 South Norwalk Boulevard, Santa Fe Springs, that engine was installed in the car with four-speed Borg-Warner gearbox.

This time, the engine was a Hi-Performance 260, further breathed upon by Shelby and Moon while it had been in their custody. Shelby would really have preferred a glassfibre body for cheapness and ease of production, but there had not been time to argue about it. Anyway, AC's supply lines

from their part-owned subsidiary, the Brownlow Sheet Metal Co, in west London, were well established, and the all-aluminium body weighed barely 50lb (22.5kg).

So still unpainted, in bare aluminium, differing visually from the Ace mainly in its small wheel-arch extensions for the wider track and bigger wheels, and a smaller grille, the first Cobra was immediately taken out by Shelby and Moon on a track test around the local oilfields.

Shelby was happy enough with the car's performance to come back and celebrate with more than one beer.

According to the Shelby American Automobile Club's *Shelby American World Registry* (which lists every Cobra ever made, and virtually every other 1960s Shelby car), CSX2000 was completed on 26 February 1962. It had the 260 motor with single carburettor, worm-and-sector steering, the inboard rear brakes, 5.5in (140mm) chrome wire wheels, and Ace-style bodywork, with the normal, long, Ace bootlid. Carroll Shelby has owned it ever since, but one of his first obligations was to show it to Dave Evans at Ford and, having seen it, Evans was apparently a happy man too.

Back in California, Pete Brock, an accomplished graphic designer on top of all his other talents, had already designed a Cobra badge, the classic stylized snake's head, although that did not appear on the prototype for a while yet. Now, he was the first regular test driver, as the car was refined over endless miles around Riverside.

It was announced to the press on 10 April 1962, shown off for the first time with its aluminium shell still unpainted but at least polished, which, according to Dean Moon took 'a dozen people and at least twenty boxes of steel wool'. Next time it appeared, it was painted a bright yellow to look its best under the lights of the Ford stand at the 1962 New York Auto Show, which opened on 21 April.

Brock's graphics gave Cobra a powerful image.

The 1953 London Show, where the Ace had been unveiled, had had that '100mph' theme; the 1962 New York Show showed that the US industry was back into the performance business. GM, with their latest Corvettes and Corvairs, and Ford, with the Corvair-baiting Falcon Sprint V8 compact, were the main protagonists, and alongside the typically garish show cars on any other

stand, the Cobra did look stunningly simple and handsome.

Next steps were to organize some magazine test exposure and to take some orders, neither of which proved to be a problem. Shelby, with his reputation as a racing driver, not to mention his Drivers' School and generally flamboyant profile, had excellent contacts with the major US motoring magazines, and they were queueing up to test the Cobra.

Unfortunately, for the moment, although Shelby had announced that production was underway and that he was taking orders, the Cobra was just that: *the* Cobra, the one-and-only.

The first magazine actually to drive it (and not surprisingly since Shelby was a 'contributing editor'), was *Sports Car Graphic*. Their test was published in May 1962, and they had driven the car in its original, raw state, even before it was painted for the New York Show. It was registered CL.10303, had hand-painted 'Shelby' scripts on its nose and tail, and small 'Powered by Ford' badges on the flanks.

It had one of the original two 260 engines. Ford had supplied the early 260 engines to Shelby in a special series with a different

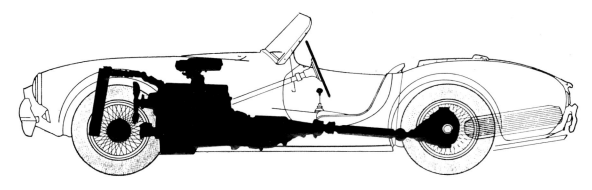

All the Cobra's major mechanical elements were within the wheelbase, giving excellent balance. The engine and gearbox were set so far back as to require only a very short propshaft.

Numerous engine options were offered right from the Cobra's announcement, up to and including full-race arrangements using four downdraught Weber carburettors, such as on this later Gurney Weslake engine.

camshaft (just one camshaft, of course, in the centre of the block), with solid rather than hydraulic cam-followers, high compression pistons, and cylinder heads with larger ports. Quoted outputs with this basic engine (numbered XHP-260-1) were 260bhp at 6,500rpm and 269lb ft of torque at 3,600rpm. In the first test car, it ran on a single four-barrel Holley carburettor and 9.2:1 compression ratio.

FIRST IMPRESSIONS

The magazine loved it, of course:

We spent a day playing with the car and can safely say that it is one of the most impressive production sports cars we've ever driven. Its acceleration, even with the much maltreated and dynamometer-thrashed single four-throat engine, can only be described as explosive and at least equal to that of the better running hot Corvettes and Berlinettas we've driven . . .

They did not include figures in their first test, but they did in a follow-up in the August issue, by which time the car had gained a coat of paint but kept the same 260bhp engine spec, in this case, a fresh engine with a slightly larger version of the single four-barrel carb. That gave similar horsepower and torque peaks, less low-down torque, but much more mid-to-top-end punch.

The figures are astonishing now and must have been almost unbelievable in 1962: on a

3.54:1 final drive, with fifth-wheel measurement because the car generated too much wheelspin to use the instruments, *Sports Car Graphic* recorded 0–60mph (0–96.5kph) in 4.1 seconds, 0–100mph (0–161kph) in 10.8 seconds and a standing quarter-mile in 12.9 seconds at 114mph (183.5kph). Their two-way maximum was 152mph (244kph) – reached in less than a mile; first gear ran to 41mph (66kph), second to 78mph (125.5kph), third to 109mph (175.5kph).

While alluding to the need for a degree of restraint, they praised the handling (on Goodyear SS racing tyres) and the brakes, and especially the fact that the car was docile and comfortable enough to be perfectly usable day to day.

In both their pieces, *Sports Car Graphic* reported on some engine options: the top 260 with 11.0:1 compression, reinforced main bearing caps and four twin-choke side-draught Weber carbs on a cross-over manifold, with 330bhp and the potential for up to 9,000rpm! They also spoke in May of homologation, already in hand to put the Cobra into the FIA's GT category as a standard car, or into Improved GTs as a modified one. Shelby was also looking to homologate with the SCCA, for B and A Production classes, respectively.

Other magazines tested the Cobra in quick succession, all with much the same awestruck enthusiasm. *Car Life* and *Road & Track* both reported 4.2 seconds to 60mph (96.5kph), and more than 150mph (241kph). In the tests, one magazine might have had a red car, one a blue one or a yellow one and, of course, there was the first test with the unpainted one. Well, in reality, all the tests were with the same car, because it was still the *only* car. Shelby simply kept repainting it between magazine outings to make it look as though production had already started. In fact, that was just about to happen.

5 Into Production: the Leaf-Spring Cars

Once the first Cobra, the uniquely inboard-braked CSX2000, had been completed, un-veiled at the 1962 New York Auto Show and drooled over by every magazine that could get their hands on it, the orders started to come in and Shelby and AC had to start filling them.

That was not as simple as it might have been with a normal mass-production model. CSX2000 was the prototype Cobra, but in many ways so were the next hundred and more cars that were delivered.

Consider some of the factors involved. The Cobra had been conceived, developed, and the first example built in around five months; the car as it went into production was tested and modified as the programme went along, learning something every time out; it was built by hand, partly in Britain, partly in America; every owner wanted

Cobra advertising always made a point of the dual identity of the car: a roadster that you could race at the weekends.

And there was no sexism at Shelby — women drove Cobras in the ads, too.

Ford did not especially want their name on the car at first, but they were happy to acknowledge where the power came from.

something very slightly different, and there were long lists of factory options for both road and racing for them to choose from; when cars did start being delivered, the feedback of information – especially on every day problems – was vastly multiplied. And so the cars changed.

The changes were rarely fundamental enough to merit a model number change. There were only really two of those through the whole life of the Cobra. Instead, the changes happened as and when they were appropriate, piecemeal, and not necessarily in strict chassis order because AC and Shelby did not always complete the cars in strict chassis order. There were changes for more performance, changes for better reliability, and sometimes changes from one supplier to another. With a car like the Cobra, this implies no shortcoming; it is just the way it had to happen.

After CSX2000, the next cars to be delivered were CSX2001 and CSX2002, with the CSX now officially meaning Carroll Shelby

Export. In the long term, the first '2' in the number part always signified a leaf-spring chassis; when the coil-spring chassis was introduced, its numbers began with a 3. Also later, COB would mean Cobra Britain (cars for sale on the home market), and COX would mean Cobra Export (for markets other than Britain or the USA), and the numerical part of their identification always began with a 6.

Eight 427-type chassis were also built with EFX prefixes for an experimental electric car, but more will be said about those later.

THE PRODUCTION COBRAS

CSX2001 and 2002 were air-freighted to the USA, 2001 arriving in New York on 19 May 1962 to be completed by Ed Hugus, Shelby's East Coast distributor in Pittsburgh, Pa, as the first customer Cobra. 2002 went straight to Shelby in California and became the first Cobra racer. It made its debut at Riverside (inevitably), in October 1962, driven by Billy Krause. It was an encouraging debut for the Cobra, a worrying day for anyone racing a Corvette.

The European 289 brochure used a bit of artistic licence to move the steering wheel to the right, and did not use Shelby's name up front.

The race was an SCCA three-hour endurance race supporting the Riverside GP. The SCCA had included an 'experimental' class, largely to cater for the still to be homologated 327 Corvette, which raced under the number 00. Shelby got Krause into the race under the same rules, with race number XP98. And Krause ran away from the opposition – new Corvette included – building up a lead of around 1½ miles in the first hour, before a rear hub failed.

Thereafter, the Cobra was a regular racer and, as we will see in a later chapter, soon became a winner. Racing also helped with the ongoing development of the production cars that were now starting to trickle through from Britain.

Car 2003 had been shipped by this time too, via Hugus, as were the next four, and eventually sent to Dearborn for Ford to study. Shelby sent it on a standby flight to save money, which was still in short supply. At that point, in spite of all the Ford and AC co-operation, Shelby reckoned to have spent as much as $40,000 of his own money on the project – money that he did not really have to spend.

A couple of other cars from the first half dozen were also shipped to Dearborn, where it seems that Ford were still toying with the idea of getting more involved in the Cobra project, perhaps even moving production in-house.

They got as far as a couple of styling exercises for an 'Americanized' body. The first was by Gene Bordinat, Ford's director of styling. It was known variously as the Cobra III, the XD Cobra or the Bordinat Cobra. It was quite a restrained design by 1960s US standards, squarer and sharper-edged than the voluptuous real thing, with a hint of original Thunderbird in the nose

Somewhere, everyone has a particular stretch of road that challenges the reflexes and tests that amalgamation of nerve and precision machinery that is the expert driver at one with a beautiful car. A brilliant vein of pavement to be savored with that catalyst of motion the thoroughbred Gran Turismo sports car! For this man, the true connoisseur of fine hand crafted automobiles, Carroll Shelby, has created the Cobra. A brilliant Anglo/American blend of the finest classic English styling, craftsmanship, comfort and road manners combined with American power, engineering, reliability and service. ☐ The Cobra's 289 cubic inch V-8 is engineered for power and lightness in the latest thin wall cast iron technique. This versatile new Ford high performance engine is truly the iron fist in a velvet glove! Smooth and docile while idling through traffic at twenty miles per hour in high gear or surging to 100 miles per hour in 10.6 seconds, the Cobra represents the best of two engineering worlds by combining the performance of a racing car with the reliability and ease of service of an American passenger car. Slicing the engine's 6500 RPM range with perfectly spaced ratios, the Cobra's rugged four speed transmission only helps to increase the brilliant power and torque curves that have made the Cobra a winner on racing circuits the world over. ☐ Arrowing through a warm desert evening at one hundred fifty plus miles per hour, or snarling up pine and snow covered mountain switchbacks, the Cobra's precision steering and supple four wheel independent suspension retain the perfection of "fine" required of a thoroughbred racing car. Conventional stopping distances become obsolete with a slight pressure on the four wheel girling disc brake system. (A firm pressure defies the laws of inertia!) Safe? Absolutely! The Cobra is a genuine Gran Turismo sports car designed and engineered to cruise above the century mark in complete comfort and security. ☐ The same careful detail evident in the engineering is reflected in the interior. The Cobra's racing heritage is comfortably evident with deep hip hugging English leather bucket seats facing a very complete instrument panel. Driver placement behind the adjustable laminated wood rim steering wheel has been carefully planned with relationship to all controls.

US (above) and British (right) advertising copy styles varied quite markedly.

profile, retractable headlights, and a big panel of louvres let into the bonnet. In its way, the two-seater roadster was pretty enough, but looking at it now it looks dated where the Cobra itself still has that totally timeless beauty.

Ford were experimenting with new materials in the Bordinat Cobra, too. It had a body made from a high-impact-resistance synthetic material called Royalex, which was moulded in one piece and then bonded onto the Cobra chassis. It would obviously have led to much bigger production numbers and a much cheaper car, but it is rather doubtful whether people would be writing about it in the 1990s as one of the great classics.

The same goes for Dearborn's other styl-ing exercise on those early chassis, a fast-back coupe version of the Bordinat roadster, known as the Cougar II. It had a few more styling extravagances: a brushed stainless-steel roof panel (à la De Lorean), and a special air vent between the rear light clusters to let high pressure air out from inside the car and prevent the low pressure outside from sucking the rear window out at high speed, which was a problem that one of the first hard-topped AC entries had had during practice for Le Mans in 1963. That was as far as either of Ford's 'in-house' Cobras ever went.

As for the Cobra itself, Ford's people, led by Dan Jones, tidied up the development loose ends, always keeping Shelby informed of what was happening, which underlines

A C COBRA

AC Cars Ltd. are pleased to announce with the co-operation of Carroll Shelby and the Ford Motor Company of America, the AC Cobra sports car.

The Cobra has already proved itself in competition in America during 1962, and was the first British car to finish during the 1963 Le Mans 24 hour race averaging 109 m.p.h. for the whole race including pit stops.

The Cobra was conceived primarily as a road and touring car, and its success in competition is a tribute to the soundness of its design, all improvements conceived under the most arduous racing conditions have been incorporated in the normal production cars and the safety factor available for normal road use is considerable.

The 4.7 litre V.8 engine which powers the Cobra is raced proved. The oversquare bore and stroke 101.6 mm. 72.9 mm. ensures low piston speed at the high crankshaft speeds obtainable by this unit. Crankshaft and connecting rod bearings are lead bronze.

The Ford Motor Company of America have developed new techniques for iron casting, and through this have been able to reduce the weight of the engine block and cylinder heads to a very considerable degree, this lightweight engine, an advanced design which pioneered the thinwall casting technique, combines extreme durability with per-formance superior to many highly stressed racing engines.

The four-speed gearbox designed by Borg-Warner provides synchromesh on all forward speeds. A.C. Cars Ltd. and Carroll Shelby have collaborated in creating the Cobra, a brilliant Anglo-American blend of classic English styling, craftsmanship, comfort, and road manners, combined with the very latest in American V.8 engine designs and techniques.

Steering is by rack and pinion and braking from speeds up to 150 m.p.h. is assured by Girling disc brakes on all four wheels. The body in the A.C. tradition is hand made in aluminium on a steel tube chassis providing great strength with lightness.

Full weather equipment is standard on the Cobra with a soft Vinyl top and sliding side windows, top and tonneau, the car is completely protected from the weather. Heater and demisters, and screen washers are standard equipment.

the nature of the working relationship that Shelby had built with Ford – a relationship based on mutual respect.

The Ford people gradually worked through the Cobra's detail problems, like the cooling system (and especially cockpit cooling), the steering, the electrical system and the instruments. Shelby says they 'did a pretty thorough job'. Getting the Cobra right meant that Ford could back it with confidence.

STARTING TO SELL

Shelby's earliest advertising for the Cobra was under the heading 'Shelby AC/Cobra Powered by Ford'. It showed the handsome show-prepared car, with chrome-plated wire wheels out in the open countryside with a young lady standing alongside and singularly inappropriately attired in an evening dress, long white gloves and a tiara! Inside, the brochure was a bit more Shelby, with a bare chassis and a car in the process of assembly. The blurb was classic American 1960s ad-speak:

Racing, touring, everyday enjoyment of a thoroughbred car, they're all yours in the new Shelby AC/Cobra. Here is a true sports-touring automobile which can actually be raced, with every expectation of success, in its normal street trim.

Yet in the city or cross-country, it remains a docile and extremely comfortable means of transportation.

The Shelby AC/Cobra achieves this often-promised-seldom-delivered ideal for one simple reason; it was designed that way. In no respect is it a compromise.

Representing the fusing of two tried and proven engineering programmes and backed by

The later European spec car shows a different, rounder wheelarch style, wing vents and a short boot lid, but loses none of the Cobra's essential simplicity of line.

One of the earliest ads for the right-hand-drive spec car, with original wheelarch style and simple overriders.

the manufacturing experience of two of the most respected automotive firms on either side of the Atlantic, the Shelby AC/Cobra has a faultless background. It has an equally exciting future.

The main copy line read 'BUY IT! . . . OR WATCH IT GO BY!'; the copy ended by exhorting 'Demand for this unique automobile is already beyond expectation. Production is limited. Order your Shelby AC/Cobra now'. And people did. Carroll Shelby, on the back of the brochure in a smart suit and tie, certainly looked like the sort of man you could buy a sports car from. The first batch of 100 cars (enough to qualify for homologation) was ordered from AC during 1962, for completion by early 1963 – for homologation purposes, of course. The first thirty or so were finished by June, seventy-five or eighty were complete by the end of the year, and the initial run was completed by April 1963. Some were completed by dealers (notably Hugus in Pittsburgh and Tasca Ford in East Providence, Rhode Island), and a lot of the cars that Shelby themselves did had competition connections, but it was soon obvious that Shelby needed more assembly space than he had at Santa

Fe Springs, where he had managed to assemble his first thirty Cobras at a rate of only around two cars a week.

The production process was labour and space intensive. At the AC end, most of the parts were made in-house, and almost entirely by hand, including the seat and hood frames. The chassis and body frames were all cut, bent and welded-up (using both arc and gas welding) in the works, starting with the main frame tubes and the crossmembers, then building upwards with the suspension and final-drive mountings and the superstructure for the body, in both round and square section tubing. Suspension, steering and brake assemblies were fitted, inner panels, bulkhead firewalls and footboxes riveted to the framework, and the electrical equipment fitted. The aluminium bodies themselves were hand-made and were riveted to the lightweight superstructure. That was more or less all – the Cobra was a very simple car. Each chassis took about four weeks to complete and AC's maximum capacity was around ten to fifteen cars a week.

Complete chassis sat in the AC showrooms while waiting to be transferred, a few cars at a time, by road to London's Victoria Docks (without engines and gearboxes, of course, and without driveshafts, because incomplete cars were subject to considerably less import duty than complete ones). They were often shipped on old Ace 'slave' wheels, turned round if necessary to give clearance for the bigger brakes. Only very urgently needed chassis (which usually meant racing or development ones) had the luxury of being flown out.

At the other end, the cars arrived at the docks waxed but not always painted, with their windscreens off and stored under a tonneau. The bare engines arrived from Ford in crates and had the ancillaries added

at Shelby, where they were also mated to alloy-cased versions of the Ford/Borg Warner four-speed manual gearbox, modified with stronger input shafts and special, closer ratios.

The alloy bodies were often damaged in transit so that they needed tidying up, but the normal build process involved de-waxing the cars, removing the bonnets, fitting water and oil temperature lines and fuel pipes, then putting the car up onto stands where three or four mechanics at a time could work on fitting the engine and transmission assembly.

Each car as it was finished was put through a 75-point check list, the engine run

A rear view of an early European car showing the long boot lid. The cockpit was little changed from the Ace, including the door pulls.

The stubby lever for the Ford/Borg Warner four-speed gearbox. The T-piece is for the reverse lock-out.

gently, and finally each and every car was tested for about thirty miles on a road route around the factory locale – much of it round a convenient new commercial site at Marina del Rey, often with Shelby driving, and with the local police apparently choosing to ignore any minor indiscretions.

The trim and paint were done last. The former always included leather-trimmed bucket seats, and full carpeting; the latter came in a choice of just two colours initially, either red or white, but was soon extended to include blue, black, green or maroon.

A fair few customers (many of them converts from Corvette or Jaguar XK) came to the works to see their own cars being completed, and the twin problems of de-

Engine dress-up parts for the road cars included ribbed aluminium rocker covers, chromed air cleaner housing and . . .

. . . chromed bumper guards.

veloping the cars as they were going along and offering so many options did not make life easier for Shelby, either.

CALLING THE OPTIONS

The race options list was obviously the most complicated. Typically it catered for safety modifications like roll hoops and competition seats, and bodywork tweaks like additional vents, an undertray, competition wind-screen and driving light kits, even a radiator stoneguard.

Chassis modifications offered for racing included brake scoops, alloy calipers, dual master cylinder, larger fuel tanks (up to a 37-gallon (168-litre) alloy type), front and rear roll-bars, competition springs and dampers, and uprated wire or alloy wheels. You could specify pretty well whatever you could think of in the engine and gearbox depart-

ment, a huge choice of inlet systems, a competition exhaust with side pipes, large capacity cooling system, various ignition system boosts and, of course, the fundamentals, eventually including such exotic items as alloy block and heads from the Ford 'Indy' engine, and a full range of high performance engine internals.

The roadgoing options and accessories list from the factory was a lot shorter than the racing one. It included mostly cosmetic and comfort add-ons – like aluminium rocker covers, chromed air cleaner, aluminium intake manifold, chromed exhaust pipe ends, chromed luggage rack, chromed front grille and rear bumper guards, adjustable wind deflectors, tinted visors, whitewall tyres, exterior mirror, an AM radio. A lift-off glassfibre hard-top was soon available, too. You could also specify competition seat belts if you wanted to look the part, and a Smiths heater. Looking at early invoices, there did

The A.C. Cobra fitted with a Fibre Glass Hard Top, designed and manufactured by A.C. Cars.

A large plastic wrap round rear view light, provides excellent all round visibility.

The COBRA Hard Top

A.C. CARS LIMITED, THAMES DITTON, SURREY, ENGLAND
Telegraphic Address: Autocarrier, Thames Ditton   Telephone: EMBerbrook 5621

Hard-top was specified as an option from the early days – not in the fastback style of the 1963 Le Mans car but in this handsome, conventional shape.

not seem to be a consistent price for the heater as an option; this really did seem to be make-it-up-as-you-go-along time.

Nobody had thought of a heater on the original spec, and depending on where a car was delivered, north or south, it could either roast or freeze its occupants; at least with the heater, northern Cobra owners could stay warm in winter.

There were cooling problems with the cars themselves, too, at first. The first cars supplied by AC had the Zephyr radiator as used on the last Ford-engined Aces, and it could not cope with a mixture of V8 capacity and California climate. For a while, Shelby fitted aluminium Corvette radiators bought incognito at Chevy dealers, which could have been embarrassing for Ford. He soon switched to a custom-built brass-cored radiator from the McCord Radiator Co, to Ford specifications, but AC supplied several more cars with Zephyr brackets, which made assembly awkward. Early cars were also fitted with the mechanical fan from the six-cylinder Falcon, to be used for the first 6000 miles as the engine loosened up and then to be replaced by an electric fan. On early cars, the exhausts emerged in front of the rear wheels; on later ones they came out below the rear bumper.

After mid-1963, wheelarches were a touch wider, to accept 6in (15cm) rather than 5½in (14cm) wheels, and side vents were standard. This is a 1965 car.

Notwithstanding all the detail variations on the early cars, the basic specifications were solidly fixed by now. The chassis was the classic Ace-type ladder, uprated as already described with the traditional transverse leaf-spring upper-link and wishbone lower-link suspension, with telescopic dampers, all clothed in a hand-made aluminium body on a 'Superleggera'-type lightweight framework. Brakes were now all outboard, 12in (305mm) Girling discs at the front, 11in (280mm) at the rear, where the Ace had only ever offered discs on the front. Steering was worm and sector, with less than a couple of turns lock to lock.

The final drive was the Salisbury unit as on the prototype, and the gearbox the Ford/Borg Warner four-speed manual, with direct top, a short lever and remote linkage. The clutch was a single dry-plate unit, hydraulically controlled.

Standard engine spec was the 3.80 × 2.87in (96.5 × 72.9mm), bore and stroke 260cu in (4261cc) all-iron pushrod overhead-valve Challenger V8, with 9.2:1 compression ratio, solid cam-followers and a Shelby-spec camshaft, and a single Holley four-barrel carburettor (slightly larger than on the first prototype) on a cast-iron manifold. The exhausts used four-into-two tubular headers.

Quoted outputs were 260bhp at 5,800rpm (1bhp per cubic inch, or 61.0bhp per litre), and 269lb ft of torque at 4,500rpm. The red-line was well beyond the quoted maximum-power revs, at 7,200rpm, and magazine testers reported that the Cobra would reach the red-line even in top.

Power was not the whole secret of the Cobra, in fact by many standards of the early 1960s in muscle-car-mad America, 260bhp was no more than modest. The Cobra was not only adequately powerful,

Nobody seemed to have thought about a heater as standard equipment for the Cobra, and there were plenty of early cooling problems under the bonnet too. This car has switches for additional electric fans.

though, it was also small and light – and that was where it took the advantage.

It was only 151.5in (384.5cm) long (not much over 12.5ft), and 61in (154.9cm) wide, on a very short, 90in (228.6cm) wheelbase, which is over 17in (43.2cm) shorter overall than on a current Porsche 911, and 4in (101mm) narrower, on almost exactly the same wheelbase. It is also very close to the Honda CRX coupe, which today looks like a very compact car indeed. Front and rear tracks were 51.5in (130.8cm) and 52.5in (133.3cm) respectively, and the Cobra usually sat on 6.40 × 15in (162 × 381mm) front and 6.70 × 15in (170 × 381mm) rear Goodyear SS tyres.

It weighed just 2,020lb (916.2kg) at the kerb. That means 288bhp per ton – better than today's Ferrari Testarossa (with 240) or Porsche Turbo (with 222), and only just behind the last of the Lamborghini Countachs (with 312bhp per ton). That power to weight figure, of course, was only the starting point for the Cobra with all its available tuning options; you did not have to spend too much to have 325bhp and 360bhp per ton on tap; and for racing you could eventually have a reliable 380bhp and chuck away even more weight.

MOVING ON

In all, completing each car took only about eight hours work at Shelby, but even so the original premises were only big enough to cope with a couple of cars a week, rather at odds with the once-declared intention to build as many as 1,000 Cobras a year. So, in

June 1962, with a little help from Ford, Shelby found bigger premises.

He only had to move as far as 1042 Princeton Drive, Venice, California, to the old Scarab factory where Woolworths heir Lance Reventlow had built his innovative but ultimately unsuccessful Scarab racing and sports cars – even Grand Prix cars. The works, with about 10,000sq ft (929sq m) of floor space (similar to AC's Thames Ditton space), were alongside the Pacific and even had some of Reventlow's machinery still installed. Before long, Shelby had around thirty-five people working at Venice, including his race mechanics, and the new factory

gave him the scope to build up to five cars a week, plus a lot more space to store his incoming engines and other parts.

Shelby inherited something more important than the works from Scarab, though, in the form of two more personnel, Ken Miles and Phil Remington.

English-born Miles was a racing driver, and one of the finest development drivers in the business. He had designed the chassis for the Scarab; he made the Cobra into a race winner; and he later did the same with the GT40.

Remington had been around racing cars for most of his life as one of the original

The engine spec could be virtually anything you liked, from 260bhp for the first 260cu in engines to around 375bhp for full-house 289 racing engine. This is a fairly typical roadgoing 289 with a single four-barrel carb.

Californian hot-rodders from the early 1930s. Like Shelby, he had flown bombers during the war (but on active service in the Pacific), and had worked for the well-known race-engine builders Traco. In the early 1950s he got involved in an earlier 'American sports car' project, with a wealthy Californian by the name of Stirling Edwards, who built half a dozen V8-powered, glassfibre-bodied sports cars over the next couple of years before Remington went off to work for the Hilborn fuel injection company.

From there, he was snapped up by Reventlow, who tried very hard to compete against the Europeans in top-class motor racing before the tax-man decided his racing was not just a hobby and forced him to give up.

Phil Remington joined Shelby as director of research and development, charged with translating the comments of testers like Miles into the metal. Shelby respected him as both an engineer and an administrator.

The other administrator on the Shelby team was Al Dowd, who was introduced to Shelby by a journalist contact late in 1963 when he had just left the US Coastguard after a twenty-year career. Dowd had raced Aces. At Shelby he was the main organizational link between Ford and AC and Shelby and lots of the race teams with Cobras, and suppliers and whoever else he needed to involve.

RUNNING CHANGES

The development people at Ford and Shelby were never short of something to do on the Cobra. Even the first production cars differed in many ways from the inboard-braked prototype. The fuel tank was moved from the old Ace horizontal position underneath the boot to a new vertical position behind the cockpit and over the rear axle. That improved the chassis balance (although the Cobra was still tail-heavy) and also made the handling more consistent whether the

tank was empty or full. It also created some space for a spare-wheel-well in the boot, under a flat floor. The bootlid itself was made slightly smaller than on the Ace, for added rear body stiffness. The body was better protected from nudges by new tubular bars (a lot neater than the Ace's old US-spec bumpers) between the usual overriders.

Standard wear for early Cobras was 15 × 5.5in (381 × 140mm), silver-painted 72-spoke wire wheels with Goodyear Blue Streak tyres (Shelby was still a Goodyear dealer!). Chrome wires were one option, and alloy wheels were always another for racing, but most owners took the standard wires.

There was a typically British soft-top, comprising a detachable frame and the material to cover it with, all held down by clips and pop-studs. The story goes that when Shelby received his first Cobra from AC he did not have the vaguest idea how to put the top up, and there were no instructions to tell him.

As launched, at $5,995 plus taxes, the first Cobra cost *less* than the last of the Ace-Bristols. Looking at early invoices, it seems that the dealer mark-up on a basic car was typically around $1,000. You could also have had a mid-range street/competition option for $6,150, or an off-the-shelf full race car for around $9,900.

To put that into perspective, the only real opposition was either major-league exotica, like the Ferrari 250GT and 400 SuperAmerica, and the Aston Martin DB4GT, or the two fastest mass-market sports cars, the Corvette and the new E-Type. The Ferraris and Astons were in a totally different price league from the Cobra, and even in their more aerodynamic coupe forms could not touch the Cobra's top speed. The Corvette (by a long way) and the E-Type (just) both undercut the Cobra on price – no AC had ever claimed to be true bargain basement. The sleek E-Type coupe could just about give the Cobra a run for top speed, but by the time the E-Type got to its top speed, the massively more accelerative Cobra would have been long gone.

That, in a nutshell, was the Cobra's long suit. It did not have the most power – the Ferraris, the Aston, the Corvette, even the first E-Type had the standard 260bhp 260 beaten there – but it did have the least weight, by far, and that meant the best power-to-weight ratio, by far. This was why nothing else on the road, at any price, could even remotely approach the Cobra's acceleration figures; and very few cars since – other than limited edition supercars like the Ferrari F40 and Porsche 959 – have been able to either. It was, quite simply, a unique offering.

Shelby's arrangement with Ford allowed him to sell the Cobra through Ford dealerships (that was a major part of the reason for Ford's involvement with the Cobra in the first place, for the image spin-off), but Shelby had to find his own Ford dealers. After the first magazine road tests appeared, the dealers were finding *him*.

THE DEALER PROBLEM

In 1964 he had 175 dealers but was planning to cut back to 100 of the 'right' type. That had proved to be a problem. For one thing, Ford did not want the Cobra to go to just any dealer, and they wanted a say in how many cars were allocated to any particular area. They mainly went for areas where Corvette sales were strongest, leaving little doubt about who the target was.

Even so, it was one thing to find space for a Cobra in the showroom, mainly for it to pull in the customers for lesser Fords, but it was something else to find a salesman capable of demonstrating a Cobra without frightening himself and/or his customer half to death, or without bending the car. At least one salesman is reported to have killed both himself and his potential customer during a demo, and one Cobra on the chassis

list was reported heavily damaged by its new owner after only 2½ miles on the clock! When the fearsome 427 came along, the problem of finding salesmen who could cope with it was really quite serious.

The first year of the Cobra in production saw several specification changes on the strength of development through experience. The first significant change came at car number 70, when the 3.54:1 final drive ratio was swapped for a 3.77:1 ratio. The original had been a bit too tall for the first engines, and the lower replacement allowed even more standing start flexibility while retaining a top speed that very few would ever use anyway, at over 140mph (225kph). When the 289 Cobra went on sale in Europe, however, it kept the more long-legged 3.54 ratio – on the basis that there were theoretically a few more places where you could use the maximum speed.

The first seventy cars had used wholly Lucas electrics; from car number 71 there was a higher capacity Ford dyamo in the system, and from car number 201 there was an entirely new electrical system, by Ford, including new wiring looms, and an alternator – changed as much for cost as for reliability, even though as a lighting manufacturer, Lucas did have an unfortunate reputation in the USA as 'The Prince of Darkness'. Instrumentation also changed at car 201, from Smiths to Stewart Warner.

AC Ace steering wheels on a very few early cars proved prone to breakage under racing conditions, so the Ace wheel was quickly replaced by a stronger wheel made specifically for the Cobra.

THE LEAF-SPRING 289

The biggest early change came at car number 76, during 1963, with the availability of a new, bigger engine from Ford. It was the Challenger 289, developed from the 260 as part of the normal Ford updating process,

Selling more mundane Fords was always part of the game.

Smiths gauges identify this as an early car; the change to Stewart Warner instruments was typical of early running changes to improve the detail design.

(Left) The common view of the Cobra for Corvette and E-Type drivers, and even Ferrari drivers, was the rapidly disappearing rear end.

Standard early wheel wear was silver-painted wires, but chrome was always an option and later the wheels were wider.

One thing that never changed was the AC logo cast into the pedals – not even on the 427.

and offered as the base V8 for the Ford full-size range for the 1964 model year. As before, the Shelby version had solid cam-followers, attacking the one weak area of the engine, a tendency to valve-float problems at high revs with the normal hydraulic lifters.

Customers who ignored the advised rev-limit frequently broke their engines; ones who respected the red-line rarely had any problems.

The new capacity was achieved by leaving the stroke at the standard 2.87in (72.9mm) and increasing the bore still further, to a full 4in (101.6mm). That gave 289cu in (4736cc) and left the short-stroke's ability to rev, while adding even more piston area – a surefire route to improved performance.

Shelby's basic 289 had an 11.0:1 compression ratio and single four-barrel carburettor. It took maximum power up to 271bhp at 6,000rpm (not quite as good as the 260's 1bhp per cubic inch) and torque up more notice-ably, to 312lb ft at 3,400rpm. It did not make the Cobra any quicker, in fact no later tests of the small-block cars ever approached the figures for the early 260 tests.

That might make one wonder about how 'standard' the spec of the original 260 test car really was, but, either way, the 289's advantage was that it did make the Cobra more flexible for the road and even more tunable for competition.

LAST OF THE LEAF SPRINGS

It did not make it any more expensive, either. Even in 1964, by which time the Cobra with its 289 engine and some impor-tant chassis changes had become known as the MkII, it was still listed at a basic price of $5,995, just as launched. That was not, in all truth, a realistic price. The Cobra had not sold in anything like the numbers that Ford and Shelby had once hoped and, although it was moving steadily, it was now far more

important to Ford for prestige and to Shelby for its racing abilities than it was to either of them for income.

That said, Shelby was not doing too badly by this stage. By late 1964 he had grown out of the Venice premises, too, he was involved with the GT40 programme and with some very hot versions of Ford's new Mustang. His turnover in 1964 was around $7½ million, around $5 million of that in car sales and tuning equipment. Ford's Total Performance image – Cobra included – had also taken their sales to new levels, and if only a few hundred of them were actually Cobras, well, that was not really the point.

In fact, AC and Shelby had built just seventy-five 260 Cobras before the switch to 289 power: sixty-two purely roadgoing 260 cars; four 'works' racers (which were subse-quently updated with 289 engines, as were a number of customer cars), one racer prepared by the factory for a private en-trant, seven racers prepared totally indepen-dently, and one 'Dragonsnake' drag-racing Cobra, which also subsequently gained a 289 engine.

The next change after the 289 was intro-duced might not have sounded so fundamen-tal, but in a way it was even more significant than the increased engine size. It came on number CSX2126, completed on 31 January 1963, and it was the first real chassis change, from the Ace's old worm-and-sector steering to the more precise rack-and-pinion.

According to the chassis lists, 2126 was considered to be a prototype and was sent to Ford in Dearborn for evaluation, CSX2127, completed on 7 March specifically for Sebr-ing, was the first 'production' Cobra with rack-and-pinion steering. The change was largely prompted by the fact that most racers wanted the precision of rack-and-pinion, not the worm-and-sector's suscepti-bility to toe-in/toe-out changes as the sus-pension rose and fell.

The modifications, which also involved

slightly shorter wishbones with more widely-spaced pivots, plus revised uprights and spring mountings, were done in Thames Ditton, by Phil Remington (who had flown out specially) and AC's Alan Turner. The rack they used came from the MG Midget parts bin, and the changes had the desired effect. The new chassis was reckoned to be a full two seconds a lap quicker around Riverside!

From car number 160, the handling was even further improved on the road cars by a switch from 5.5in (140mm) to 6in (152mm) rims with suitably wider Goodyear G8 tyres. There were subtly wider wheel arches to cover them, louvres in the front wings, for additional cockpit cooling (as first tried on the 1963 Le Mans cars), and a return to a slightly larger grille opening for better engine-bay cooling. From car number 164, the single brake master cylinder was changed for a dual one and, from number 187, the manually adjustable handbrake layout was changed for a self-adjusting one – all just tidying up the details, really.

A COBRA FOR EUROPE

By this time, specifications were becoming a bit more standarized, but the Cobra still was not on sale in Europe. It had made European show appearances in both Paris and London during 1962 alongside the Ace and the Aceca, which were still in production. The grey show car with blue leather interior was car number CSX2025, and it was a left-hand-drive car.

The first right-hand-drive Cobra was chassis number CS2030, dropping the X because it was not intended for export. It was retained by AC Cars, with a '4.5-litre' engine. Shelby American credited AC for the car, which was registered 300 PK on 1 November 1962 and used as the Thames Ditton demonstrator. One person it was demonstrated to was Stirling Moss, who was photographed sitting in the car in London, talking to Charles and Derek Hurlock.

The first British test of a Cobra appeared in *Autosport* in June 1963, when John Bolster had a long day on British roads with Carroll Shelby's own early left-hand-drive 289 (with temporary registration QQ 907).

The next right-hand-drive cars were CSX2130 (the unraced 1963 Le Mans prototype) and CS2131 (dropping the X again, because it was never intended for export; there was also a CSX2131, which was an AC coupe, along the lines of the Daytona, of which more in the competition chapter). CS2131 was one of two AC Cars entries at Le Mans in 1963, prepared by John Willment and driven by Ninian Sanderson and Peter Bolton to finish third in the GT category and seventh overall.

Apart from that, you could not actually buy a right-hand-drive Cobra in Europe until late in 1963. It was AC who introduced the European cars, built completely in Thames Ditton, including fitting the engines and all running gear, with COX6 numbers for European export cars and COB6 numbers for British domestic market cars (which also meant right-hand drive). The first three European Cobras went to France, the fourth car was sold in Britain in November 1963 to Lord Cross, who raced it extensively; and the next (the second right-hand-drive 'production' Cobra) was used as a works demonstrator. Initially, there was just to be a run of a dozen right-hand-drive cars, because AC were fully occupied in building chassis for Shelby. Cobras were not properly available in the UK until around September 1964.

As launched here, the 289 Cobra cost £2,030, plus taxes, which was expensive compared to the opposition, and probably a bit too late for the Cobra to have the same sort of impact it had had a couple of years before in the USA. As a European car it did not have the advantages of instant parts availability as in the USA, or of low US fuel costs for the relatively thirsty V8s.

47 COB, chassis number COX6011, started life as a show car in Geneva and was changed from left- to right-hand drive when it came back to England in 1970.

Only sixty-one European-spec leaf-spring Cobras were built, the last of them in mid-1965, by which time a new and even more spectacular breed of Cobra was emerging from Shelby's workshops. This one had undergone a metamorphosis from the old Ace-based transverse-leaf-spring chassis to a more modern coil-spring layout, and it opened up a new phase in the Cobra's career with a mighty new option, the 427 engine.

6 Coil Springs and the Mighty 427

In March 1964, Ken Miles, the man who had probably spent more racing and testing time in Cobras than anyone else in the world, appeared at Sebring with a new car that even his prodigious talent was clearly having trouble in taming.

Even during practice, Miles – who was due to share the car with Shelby American mechanic John Morton – spun off the circuit while going through the Esses, and somehow managed to connect with the only tree within several miles on Sebring's bare landscape. The car was repaired overnight and Miles raced it, but he did not finish – he retired when the motor threw a connecting rod.

It was no ordinary Cobra that had seemingly got the better of Miles that day. CSX2166 had started life in July 1963 as a red 289 street car with black leather interior, nothing more out of the ordinary than that. In March 1964, though, when the car appeared at Sebring, the normal 289 engine had gone and in its place was a 427cu in (6,997cc) Ford NASCAR racing engine and 'top-loader' racing transmission. It was a long way from a production possibility, even for homologation, but it was a sign of the way Shelby was thinking.

The reason for an even more potent Cobra was simple: competition. From day one the Cobra had been a formidable racer, and from around days two and three it had been a formidable racer that increasingly stayed in one piece for long enough to take the chequered flag.

By mid-1963, the 289s had won every-thing worth winning in US domestic racing, and were virtually unbeatable in USRRC and SCCA Production racing, but Carroll Shelby had ambitions for the Cobra far beyond that. He was still out to get Ferrari in the manufacturers' Championship.

GOOD – BUT NOT GOOD ENOUGH

The Cobra had been homologated by the FIA for international racing by the start of the 1963 season, to contest the GT category of the FIA World Manufacturers' Championship. By seaon's end, the Cobras (with committed Ford support) had had a few reasonable results, including their first FIA race win, but certainly not enough to qualify as 'ass-whipping'. In the early days, they still had the bad combination of being quick but breakable, and for European-style racing on longer, faster circuits, the brick-like aerodynamics of the roadsters meant that for all their light weight and ample power they were not actually quick enough to beat Ferrari's coupes – not even when the 289 arrived.

The details can wait until we look at the Cobra's racing history but, basically, Shelby attacked the lack of maximum speed with better aerodynamics in 1964, via the Daytona coupe. The Daytona came so close to winning the 1964 GT Championship, but was beaten in the end with the last-minute help of another piece of Ferrari's traditional political chicanery.

Ken Miles (left) was the man who made the 427 work.

That had been 1964. Shelby knew that for 1965, the opposition would be even stronger: Ferrari looked set to homologate a 275LM; Ford would have the GT40 (which would mean a lot less corporate enthusiasm for the Cobras and Daytonas); and on the home front Chevrolet would supposedly have a new 396cu in (6,494cc) racing engine for their lightweight Grand Sport Corvettes. Something less than 400bhp absolute maximum from a reliable full-race 289 was not going to be enough; hence the monstrous 427 giving Miles a hard time around Sebring.

In a way, Miles had mainly himself to blame. The 427 was largely his own concept, kicked over first towards the end of 1963 when it became clear that the opposition – Ferrari in Europe, GM at home – would soon be moving the goalposts with bigger engine options and a lot more power. Ford's 427

NASCAR engine was an all-too-obvious temptation for a man like Miles, who had virtually been brought up on parts-bin engineering.

THE FIRST 427s

The first manifestation was very rough and ready. CSX2166's chassis had been given some modest strengthening but no major redesign beyond rejigging the engine mounts. It was clothed in a patchily lashed-up shell, with tack-on arches (to cover the wider rubber and the Halibrand pin-drive wheels demanded by around 485bhp), and a lot of hastily cut holes and scoops around the nose to keep it cool.

Miles tested it briefly around Riverside, and then took it for that inauspicious debut

Ken Miles (1918–1966)

Carroll Shelby's competition manager cum development engineer, Ken Miles, was one of the finest assets the Cobra project ever had. Widely acknowledged throughout the racing world as one of the finest test drivers in the business, Miles also had the engineering and design skills to convert what he learned on the track into positive advances in the car – or the ability to communicate both problems and solutions to those he worked with.

Like the Cobra, he was an Anglo-American. He was English born, on 1 November 1918 in Sutton Coalfield, near Birmingham. Between the wars he started a competition career on motor cycles, and became a tank sergeant in the army. After World War II he switched from two wheels to four, going vintage racing with an Alfa-Romeo, an Alvis and a Bugatti before starting to make a name for himself with a Ford V8-powered Frazer-Nash – second cousin to the Ace with its Bristol engine connection, and forerunner of the Cobra philosophy once the Ford V8 was installed.

In 1952, Miles moved to California. He took up racing again almost immediately, initially with a standard MG TD. He was disqualified from his first race, at Pebble Beach, for reckless driving. The brakes on his MG had failed but he carried on regardless, with barely reduced lap times.

It was at Pebble Beach, in 1953, that he started a run of fourteen consecutive wins with a tube-framed MG special, just the sort of thing that was leading up to the Ace back in Britain.

From 1954, 'Mr MG' drove an MG TF while he was building another infamous MG special that came to be known as the Flying Shingle. In 1955, he also drove a Triumph TR3 and from 1956 he started a successful association with all sorts of Porsches, including another hybrid, a Porsche-engined Cooper dubbed, inevitably, the Pooper.

He drove Porsches of one sort or another, and with successes even against the works cars, right up to the 1960s. In 1961 he had a less impressive time with a Maserati but began to work as a test driver for Sunbeam, on the Alpine. (He later worked with Shelby to develop the Ford V8-engined Sunbeam Tiger, a truly mass-produced Anglo-American hybrid that never quite had the charisma of the Cobra, but was a pretty good car in its own right).

Miles arrived at Shelby via Lance Reventlow's Scarab operation, when Shelby moved into the old Scarab works after Reventlow had been forced to admit defeat. Reventlow, son of Woolworth heiress Barbara Hutton, had failed partly because his front-engined GP cars, although exquisitely engineered, were outdated by the time they got to Europe, and partly because the tax-man finally decided that his car building was a business and not a hobby. Miles had worked as a consultant for Reventlow, and designed the Scarab chassis, a lot more complex than the Cobra's, but along similar lines of tubular frame, alloy body and big V8 engine.

The lean, hawk-nosed Miles was not an easy man to know: he spoke his mind, often quite forcibly, with a British accent and usually out of the side of his mouth; he did not think much of people who did not listen to what he was saying, yet he was usually smiling so long as he was around racing cars. He got on well with Shelby's small organization because he was working with like-minded, capable people, with virtually no red-tape at all.

As well as the 289 and 427 Cobras and, of course, the Daytona, Miles worked with Shelby on the Tiger, the Shelby Mustangs, and with Ford and Shelby on the GT40, the Ford MkII and the J-Car. He raced the GT40 family extensively, too, winning a lot of races.

In the end, his job claimed his life. Testing the latest GT40 J-Car at Riverside on 17 August 1966, he lost control, crashed heavily and was killed.

outing at Sebring, where even the most casual observer could not miss noticing the surplus of power over traction.

It did not kill Miles's enthusiasm, though, and a good deal of work went into the next 427 pre-prototype, as based on another 1963 289 chassis, number CSX2196.

Strictly speaking, this was originally neither 289 nor 427; Miles fitted it first with a full-race all-alloy 390cu in (6,391cc) Ford

V8 engine, running on four downdraught Weber carburettors to give 427-type power with 289-type weight, because full-race 427 engines were in short supply.

The weight-saving was extended to the chassis, to the extent of throwing away all the interior panelling from the body and, of course, all the trim. All-up weight came down to barely 1,600lb (725.5kg), which promised formidable performance with not far short of 500bhp. Given that the car was still suspended on leaf springs, it did not promise much by way of manners.

As an experimental car, Miles equipped it with almost standard-shaped Cobra bodywork, but split the shell across the middle and hinged it at nose and tail, to lift easily in two sections and give instant access to engine and chassis. In public, the car was known as the 'Flip-Top'; in private, it was known by Shelby people as 'The Turd'.

By the time it appeared at Nassau in December 1964, it had a full 427 engine. In short, the car disappeared into the distance from the opposition (including the lightweight Grand Sport Corvettes) on that first outing, but only went two thirds race distance before being sidelined by a chassis breakage. The two prototypes had done enough to prove their potential, though, and Shelby decided to pursue the 427 route.

Of course, if the Cobra with 427-power was still going to be eligible for FIA racing, it would have to qualify first as a production car – and that meant 100 examples again. Which in turn meant that the 427, however rabid, would eventually have to be a customer car too.

There was a little way to go before that could happen. The racers that Miles had built really had been almost undrivable. The 427 engine, rather than the exotic and rare alloy 390, was going to be the production engine choice, but it was quite obviously way too powerful for the existing transverse-leaf-spring chassis.

It was a monster of an engine, and not just by way of its capacity. That in itself was extreme enough for a car which started with 'only' 260cu in (4,261cc), but as well as the capacity, the 427 was virtually an out-and-out racing engine. More precisely, it was a NASCAR engine, and NASCAR was all about maximum horsepower.

THE BIG-BLOCKS

The 427 'big-block' line dated back to 1958, when it started with the 352cu in (5,768cc) V8. For 1960, Ford had uprated the 352 with some classic performance options: solid cam followers instead of the original hydraulics; higher compression; better exhaust manifolding, and a four-barrel Holley carburettor on an aluminium manifold that also gave a weight saving of around 50lb (22.5kg). It was one of Ford's first no-compromise high-performance engines, and the first Ford V8 to produce more than 1bhp per cubic inch, with 360bhp on tap.

For Ford's full-size 1961 models, to whit the Galaxies, and for the sporting Thunderbird, the engine grew to 390cu in (6,391cc) by increasing its stroke from 3.50 to 3.78in (88.9 to 96.0mm). It became a long-running engine in the Ford catalogue, and a versatile one. In base form it started with 'economy' two-barrel carburation and just 250bhp, or by 1961 you could have anything from 300bhp to 401bhp, the latter with the dealer-installed option of triple two-barrel carburettors.

To get your 401bhp 390, you started with the Thunderbird Special engine, factory equipped with a single four-barrel Holley on a cast-iron manifold with 9.6:1 compression. That gave 300bhp at 4,600rpm and 427lb ft of torque at a slogging 2,800rpm. The Thunderbird Special High Performance V8 was the next possibility, with a bigger four-barrel Holley on an aluminium manifold, tubular-type exhaust manifolds, a better camshaft, solid cam followers, and 10.6:1

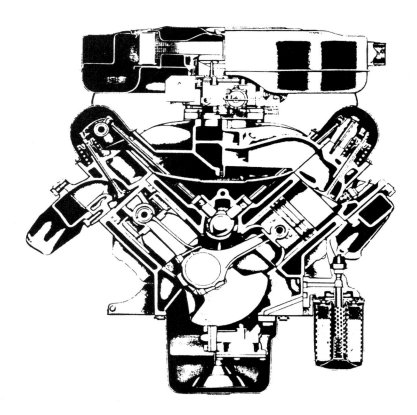

A typical cross-section of one of Ford's 'big-block' V8 engines, the basis of both 427 and 428 Cobra engines.

compression. That gave 375bhp at 6,000rpm and 427lb ft of torque at 3,000rpm. And if you wanted the real top-of-the-shop option, the dealer took the (6V) triple two-barrel Holley induction as shipped to special order in the boot, bolted that on and gave you 401bhp at 6,000rpm and 430lb ft of torque at 3,500rpm.

Another big forward step in Ford's Total Performance image came with this engine, in the availability (again as a dealer-installed option) of the Borg-Warner T10 four-speed manual transmission. That was light years ahead of Ford's stodgy Cruise-O-Matic auto and the old three-speed-plus-overdrive manual; it was also the gearbox that went into the first Cobras, behind the 'small-block' 260 engine.

That is how Ford were progressing in the early 1960s as Total Performance took hold: 'Speed costs money, how fast do you want to go?', as the sign over one American engine tuner's door used to read.

For the 1962 model year, you could go faster still as Ford settled into the horsepower race with a vengeance. The 'small-block' 260, as used in the first Cobras, was introduced, and big-block engine size went up again, to 406cu in (6,653cc). It was the first Ford Division engine ever to go over 400cu in (6,560cc), and just the thing to keep up with the latest Chevy Impala SS, Plymouth Sport Fury, Pontiac Grand Prix and Dodge Polara 500. You did not have to look far to see what image sold cars in America in 1962.

The 406 Thunderbird Special V8 was Ford's weapon for NASCAR now that Henry II had announced that Ford would no longer be shy about going racing. It had a stronger bottom end, started with a 385bhp single four-barrel version and went up to a triple two-barrel, (6V) version, with the usual niceties like solid cam-followers, aluminium inlet manifold, trick cam and high compression – now 11.4:1. With 405bhp at 5,800rpm and 448lb ft of torque at 3,500rpm it was Ford's most powerful production engine to date. But only until the 1963 season, when Ford went for broke in NASCAR, with new, more aerodynamic body shapes for the racing Galaxies and even more power. Aerodynamics had let Ford down in 1962; it certainly would not for 1963, and nor would power as the definitive version of the 427 grew out of the 352, 390, 406 progression.

The massively imposing 427 was a bigger car all round than the 289, and was aggressively rounded and purposeful, especially in this S/C form.

Even in the wider chassis and body combination, Ford's mighty Y-block 427 NASCAR-based engine was a tight fit.

It is virtually impossible to read any description of a Ford 427-engined car without finding adjectives like 'awesome', 'fearsome', 'monstrous'. Wedge-shaped combustion chambers gave good swirl characteristics, and big rectangular ports gave excellent breathing. Capacity (nominally, at least) had gone up to 427cu in (6,997cc) with still oversquare bore and stroke dimensions of 4.24 × 3.78in (101.6 × 96.0mm). With solid lifters, 11.5:1 compression, and two Holley 780cfm four-barrel carburettors on an aluminium manifold, this glorious engine produced 425bhp at 6,500rpm and 480lb ft of torque at 3,500rpm in its top street specification, and with plenty more available for any racing class that allowed further tuning.

It was also an extremely strong engine, with a forged steel crankshaft running in cross-bolted main bearings with high-strength connecting rods all designed to keep it in one piece during high-load operation. It had very large oil galleries, good for both lubrication and cooling, and in 'side-oiler' form the oil feed to the main bearings came in from the side rather than from below, for even more reliable lubrication under heavy cornering forces.

In not far short of two tons of Galaxie 500, even its 425bhp street-trim output gave staggering performance and this was the engine that Shelby and Miles were now introducing into barely half that bulk of Cobra.

A CHASSIS TO MATCH THE POWER

So with the 427, the Cobra had a whole catalogue of problems to face. It was physically a much larger engine than the beautifully compact 289. It was of the old 'Y-block' school in which the crankcase extended below the crankshaft centre line. It was heavy – almost 200lb (90.5kg) heavier than the 289. It naturally needed a lot more cooling and a lot more carburation. And its massive power (and especially torque) figures were finally more than the old Ace-based chassis could cope with. So, at last, it was redesign time.

It would be the first time that Shelby had effectively been able to start from scratch on a Cobra design, and although his budget, as usual, would be tight, he would have full technical support from Ford. He had just signed a five year co-operative deal with them, a 'reciprocal technical and marketing assistance agreement', which included the

Shelby Mustang and Ford GT40 production programmes.

So, by the time Shelby and Ford and AC had finished with the 427 Cobra, about the only thing that was left over was the basic layout.

Shelby's project engineer, Jim Benavides, started with the familiar ladder, but a much more substantial ladder. The main frame tubes were made from yet thicker-gauge material and increased in diameter from 3in to 4in (which was reckoned to make them three times stronger). They were also moved about five inches further apart, and the fabricated-sheet suspension towers were replaced by tubular structures.

That was only the start; the bigger chassis was given a completely new and much more modern suspension layout, too, finally aban-

The 427 chassis was virtually all new, turning to modern ideas at last with double wishbone and coil-spring suspension all round. The car was still as compact as it could possibly be.

doning the old transverse-leaf-spring upper links for a classic coil-spring/damper and double-wishbone layout. Classic, that is, on racing cars, but still very rare on a road car in the early 1960s.

By 1964, science was starting to creep into race car design, and where the old Ace had been designed on Tojeiro's garage floor, a lot of the 427 started life on Ford's computers.

The basic four-link layout, with integral coil-spring/damper units, had been worked out at Ford Engineering by Ford's Klaus Arning, who also worked on the GT40. It was schemed originally for a Mustang prototype but was an obvious choice for the 427. The basics were refined by Ford's Bob Negstadt, using the computer to optimize the pick-up points to give longer, softer suspension travel with the right degree of anti-dive and anti-squat, and to keep the tyres a lot more vertical a lot more often than had ever been possible with the old leaf springs.

There was one minor practical snag in so far as the computer's 'ideal' set-up would have placed some of the rear suspension pick-ups somewhere in the middle of the driver's bottom, but that was eventually sorted out by the engineers, who knew a bit more about practical compromises than the computer did.

The original Salisbury diff, amazingly, proved quite capable of handling the massively increased torque, but the driveshafts

The essential twin-tube layout was still recognizable, but everything on the 427 was bigger and stronger, as seen on this virtually identical 428 chassis.

'Like a 289 on steroids.'

were substantially upgraded. They had sliding splines, but even with quite long suspension travel now allowed, they underwent virtually no change in length. That was just as well, according to Miles, as the torque would almost certainly have caused any available splined drive to bind anyway. Larger, stronger hubs were used, with taper bearings, and larger brakes could be specified on competition cars. The suspension was Rose-jointed, racing-style, to be fully adjustable, and would eventually offer bronze bushes for competition or less harsh-riding rubber bushes for the road.

Finally, Negstadt and Phil Remington

(with Ford/Shelby admin-man Ray Geddes) went to AC and put in a lot of hours with AC's chief engineering designer, Alan Turner, to make the new chassis and suspension work.

In the end, it did work. It was tested at Silverstone while the Ford and Shelby personnel were still in Britain. At that stage, it was fitted with a Ford-supplied experimental engine in quite a high degree of tune with a Holley 'double-pumper' four-barrel carburettor (that is, one with two accelerator pumps) on a 'medium riser' manifold. The taller the manifold, the straighter the inlet tract and the better the maximum power but, in general, the worse the flexibility; low rise was normal street equipment, high rise was for NASCAR and drag-racing, medium rise was somewhere in between.

The original plan, from around August 1964, had been to build four coil-spring prototypes, referred to internally as Cobra IIs. The first three were going to be roadsters, looking very similar to the 289; the fourth was planned as a coupe, along Daytona lines. Cars one, three and four were originally schemed around all-alloy 390 engines, number two around the cast-iron 427, and the programme was due to be completed by November 1964.

In the event, by October the plans had been revised, extending the completion date to December. But the last two prototypes, including the coupe, did not materialize and

Additional cooling ducts in the nose and two big electric fans help control underbonnet temperature.

AC actually only built two cars designated as 427 prototypes: CSX3001 and CSX3002. They were originally numbered CSX2701 and 2702, and built as chassis only, while waiting for the body bucks to be finished. The numbers were changed when it was decided that coil-spring chassis cars should be distinguished by a number starting with a figure 3.

A COBRA ON STEROIDS

The prototypes had already been all but completed while the decision-making was going on, and they were airfreighted to Shelby in October 1964, the first one going via Ford in Dearborn who were obviously keen to have a proper look, too. Both were built to racing specs, and 3002 became the only 'works' 427 racer, being raced in SCCA events as a test-bed. The engine spec for these cars prescribed a lightweight 427 side-oiler, with aluminium heads, water-pump housing, inlet manifold, timing-chain cover, and radiator header-tank, all designed to keep engine weight down to around 565lb (256kg).

The 427 still looked like a 289 Cobra – Shelby had finally resisted any temptation to go for a Daytona-type aerodynamic car – but it looked like a 289 Cobra on steroids. Only the doors and the boot and bonnet lids were the same as on the original, everything else was scaled up. It still sat on the same, short 90in (228.6cm) wheelbase, but the 427 was wider in both body (almost entirely in the wings to accommodate much larger wheels and tyres) and track, and it was a little longer and a little heavier.

It was not heavier by much. The chassis had put on maybe 50lb (22.5kg) and in its lightest form, with the alloy sump, timing-chain cover and inlet manifold, a 427 engine was only about 150lb (68kg) heavier than a 289, and a good 150bhp stronger.

The cooling problem had been attacked with a redesigned nose, very similar in shape to the 289's, but with a bigger main grille opening with just a simple bar across the middle (SCCA said you had to race with the original grille), and a separate scoop below, for the oil-cooler on competition cars.

There were also supplementary vertical openings on either side of the grille, just below and inboard of the headlights. On road cars they would be for cockpit cooling, on full-race cars they would be ducted to provide brake cooling. The huge flip-filler for the big new fuel tank in the boot was now in the centre of the rear deck panel. There was a bit more room in the cockpit with the wider shell, but the pedals had had to be offset to the left to make room in the centre for the bigger transmission tunnel.

Naturally, 425bhp and more demanded more rubber on the road. The 427 was given 8.15 × 15in (207 × 381mm) Goodyear Blue Spot tyres – and 7.5in (190mm) wide, GT40-style, Halibrand, six-spoke, peg-drive wheels, with three-eared knock-on spinners, were standard at first. They were specially made for the 427, normally finished in black, with polished rims and polished edges to the air slots.

All in all, the 427 Cobra looked like a very mean beast indeed, and of course it was, but it was about to run into problems.

THE HOMOLOGATION SAGA

In theory, the first 100 427s should have been completed by late April 1965 to qualify for FIA homologation into the GT category, alongside the Ferrari 275LM that was Shelby's main perceived target. To that end, Shelby commissioned the first 100 427s as outright competition cars.

He could have taken a short-cut and topped up the numbers with road cars right from the start, but that was not his way of doing things. Having been so scathing about

Take away the more extreme competition fittings and the 427 still has the grace of the old Ace.

Ferrari's political manipulation of the FIA rules in Europe, and particularly in the sports and GT classes, he was not about to compromise on what he saw as a matter of principle.

Unfortunately, that meant that when the FIA inspectors arrived at Shelby's new Los Angeles airport premises on 29 April, there were only fifty-one completed 427s for them to inspect, so homologation was withheld. Only at that point did Shelby extend the build programme to include road cars, abandoning the rest of the initial run of 100 pure competition cars in the process. It was only a minor consolation to Shelby that Ferrari had failed to build enough 275s for homologation, too, so both would be competing with last year's models. Or that the SCCA were not quite so hard to satisfy, and had already

granted the 427 homologation before the end of 1964, purely on the strength of the prototypes.

Almost simultaneously with turning down the 427's first application, in June 1965, the FIA gave the situation a new twist when they announced a change in homologation requirements for the following year, for a new category to be called 'Competition GT', which would replace the existing full production GT class. It would require only fifty cars to be built, which, in theory, opened the door for the 427 in Europe for 1966, but unfortunately put it into the same class as Ford's new GT40.

That would have given Shelby, who was also, of course, deeply involved in the GT40 programme, a major political dilemma with Ford had it not been for the fact that the 427,

Hood scoops and additional cooling ducts, including non-standard ones, proliferated on competition 427s. The filler is for the oil tank.

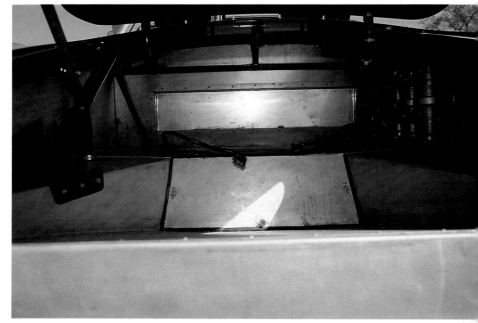

The fuel pump array on the right side of the boot of the S/C 427 hints at the engine's prodigious thirst.

The huge flip-up filler cap for quick pit action.

Halibrand pin-drive magnesium wheels were meant to be standard equipment but supplies were short.

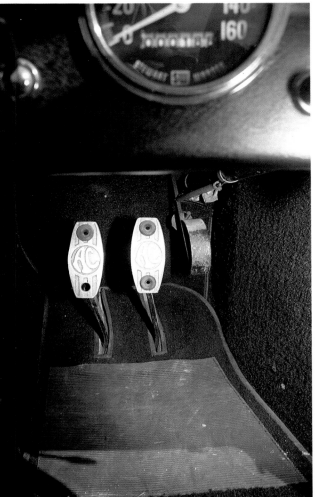

A big new drivetrain and a wider chassis centre meant the pedals were heavily offset, but still had the AC logo!

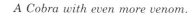

A Cobra with even more venom.

SPORTS CAR

ENGINE

Water-cooled V-8, with cast iron block, 5 main
   bearings
Bore & stroke . . . . 4.24 x 3.78 in, 107 x 96 mm
Displacement . . . . .427 cu in, 6998 cc
Compression ratio . . . . .10.4 to one
Carburetion . . . . .Two 4-bbl Holley
Valve gear . . . . .Pushrod-OHV
Horsepower (SAE) . . . . .425 bhp @ 6000 rpm
Torque . . . . .480 ft-lbs @ 3700 rpm
Electrical system . . .12-volt battery, alternator
Fuel recommended . . . . .Premium only
Mileage . . . . .9-12 mpg
Range on 18-gallon tank . . . . . .162-216 miles

CHASSIS

Wheelbase . . . . .90 in
Track . . . . .F 56, R 56 in
Length . . . . .156 in
Width . . . . .68 in
Height . . . . .49 in
Ground clearance . . . . .4.35 in
Dry weight . . . . .2354 lbs
Curb weight . . . . .2529 lbs
Test weight . . . . .2890 lbs

Weight distribution front/rear 48/52%
Pounds per bhp (test weight) 5.95
Suspension F: Ind., unequal-length wishbones
   with anti-dive and anti-squat, coil springs
Suspension R: Ind., unequal-length wishbones
   with anti-dive and anti-squat, coil springs
Brakes . . . . disc, 11.63-in front, 10.75-in rear,
   580 sq in swept area
Steering . . . . .Rack and pinion
Tires . . . . .8.15 x 15 Goodyear Blue Dot
Wheels . . . . .7½ x 15 cast alloy
   pin drive, knock-off hub

DRIVE TRAIN

Clutch . . . . .11.5-inch single dry plate,
   hydraulic release
Transmission . . . . .4-speed, all synchro

Gear	Ratio	Over-all	mph/1000 rpm	Max mph
Rev	2.32	8.21	9.86	69
1st	2.32	8.21	9.86	69
2nd	1.69	5.98	13.54	95
3rd	1.29	4.57	17.71	124
4th	1.00	3.54	22.91	160

Salisbury limited slip differential
Final drive ratio . . . . .3.54 to one

*Shelby advertised road and competition cars side by side with spec variations
as listed.*

COBRA 427
POWERED BY FORD

COMPETITION

All "Sports" specifications apply except as follows:

BODY CONSTRUCTION
Aluminum panels, large diameter lightweight steel tube frame carrying suspension mounts.

ENGINE
Water cooled V-8, with cast iron block, magnesium intake manifold, alloy cylinder heads, lightweight valves and alloy water pump.

Bore & stroke . . . . 4.24 x 3.78 in
Displacement . . . . 427 cu in
Compression ratio 12.4:1
Horsepower . . . . 480 @ 6500 rpm
Torque . . . . 510 ft-lbs @ 3700 rpm
Carburetion . . . . 4 V Holley
w/center pivot float bowls

STANDARD GEAR RATIO
4th 1:1
3rd 1.29:1
2nd 1.69:1
1st 2.32:1

CLUTCH
Ford, single plate, 11.5 in diameter

STANDARD REAR AXLE RATIO
3.77 to one

WHEELS
7½ x 15 front, 9½ x 15 rear, alloy

TIRES
Front, 9.90 x 15 Speedway Specials
Rear, 11.90 x 15 Speedway Specials

CAPACITIES
Radiator . . . . .20 quarts
Engine Oil . . . . .13 quarts wet sump—
14 quarts dry sump
Fuel Tank .42 gallons
w/dual electric fuel booster pumps
Sway bars front and rear, special tuned exhaust system, roll-over protection, seat belts, rear axle oil cooler and pump, engine oil cooler, all standard equipment.

OPTIONAL EQUIPMENT
Optional gear and rear axle ratios; special racing bucket seat, shoulder harness, quick change brake pad kit, mechanical chronometric tachometer, dry sump kit, competition windscreen.

The cockpits of competition and S/C 427s tended to be bespoke, but ex-John Woolfe S/C is typically neat and to the point. The huge gearshift is actually similar to the donor saloon's but reversed.

for all its power, really would not have had a prayer anyway of competing against the hugely more sophisticated mid-engined Ford and indeed against the comparable Ferraris. That, at a stroke, was both the beginning and the end of the 427's potential as a works racer. It was almost, in fact, the end of the 427 altogether, and almost the end of the Cobra.

The first 427 production cars, and thus the first coil-spring production Cobras, were shipped to the USA in January 1965. The

last leaf-spring cars for the US market were completed in November 1964, although leaf-spring chassis were made for European consumption (with 289 power, of course, not 427) right into mid-1965. The coil-spring, 427/428-engined 'MkIII' became available in

As with the 289, engine specs could be virtually whatever a customer wanted. This is a genuine 427 with two four barrels; milder-mannered 428-engined cars were still labelled 427.

Europe, too, from late in 1965, and when Shelby did not need the chassis at all any more, AC finally offered coil-spring 289 cars right at the end of the Cobra's career, but only ever made twenty-seven of them. Back in mid-1965, though, having tried for homologation and missed, Shelby had a yard full of around forty unsold 427 Cobras.

About a dozen of the original 'homologation' batch had been sold to private owners, to campaign mainly in SCCA production racing where they were, of course, already eligible. Shelby decided to keep back enough of the remaining cars to satisfy the FIA inspectors in November that enough 427s had been built for the new homologation requirement for 1966, for the 'Competititon GT' category.

Even completion of those cars was slow, held up by parts supply problems and by pressure of work on Shelby from the GT40 build programme, but they were homologated in November for FIA eligibility from 1 January 1966.

By November, however, Shelby had only sold about sixteen 427 cars in total, and the rest were becoming a bit of an embarrassment. There were fewer racers around who could afford a 427 than could have afforded the 289, and fewer still who could hope to drive one effectively. And, of course, there was no European market at all, because the 427 still was not eligible for FIA-sanctioned international racing until at least 1966.

THE SEMI-COMPETITION IDEA

It was one of Shelby's management people who came up with an answer. Charles Beidler, the eastern sales manager, saw the

This early Shelby 427 road car has Sunburst wheels, conventional exhaust routing and rectangular rear lights.

cars at the works, unpainted and mostly standing up on blocks because of a shortage of Halibrand pin-drive wheels. They were barely trickling out of the factory, just one at a time being completed occasionally to individual order.

Beidler suggested completing the rest to an only slightly milder specification and advertising them as the fastest production cars in the world. Thus was born the idea of the 'Semi-Competition' 427 Cobra. And the idea worked. Three more cars of the original batch were sold as full-house racers, and the remaining thirty-one were sold as 427 S/Cs, the official designation.

The first to be called an S/C was CSX3015, which had been completed in January 1965 and had been sitting around at Shelby's ever since it was airfreighted there early in the year. In December, it was described as '65 per cent complete', and earmarked for shipping back to Britain, to Ford Advanced Vehicles in Slough. Eventually, it became one of the two 'ultimate' Cobras, this one owned by Shelby, the second (CSX3303) owned by Bill Cosby.

These two had 427 engines plus two-stage Paxton supercharging, and Ford T6 heavy-duty three-speed automatic transmissions. In February 1968, Shelby's car, claiming around 800bhp (yes, eight *hundred* horsepower), recorded 0–60mph (96.5kph) in 3.8 seconds, 0–100mph (161kph) in 7.9 seconds, and a standing-start quarter-mile in 11.9 seconds, with a terminal speed of 116mph (186.5kph), for *Road & Track* magazine. They did not actually try a maximum speed run but suggested that something over 180mph (289.5kph) seemed likely.

The 'production' S/Cs of the main series were not quite as manic as that, but they were mighty quick. Most magazines tested 'street' 427s and typically quoted top speed at about 165mph (265.5kph) and recorded 0–60mph (96.5kph) times around 4.2 seconds (or in one case four seconds dead). Generally, 0–100mph (161kph) was claimed

in around nine or ten seconds, and standing quarter miles in the very low 12 second range at close to 120mph (193kph). One of the most oft-quoted figures was Miles's ability to run 0–100mph (161kph) and back to a stop in 13.8 seconds.

That said, though, most testers commented on just how docile the 427 felt, even alongside a 289. That was mainly because of the carburation on the street cars; the four-barrel Holleys had relatively small primary chokes, which gave that docile flexibility around town, but enormous secondary chokes, which instantly gave a massive horsepower and torque boost if the throttle was snapped all the way open. Several magazines commented that it was wise to have the 427 in an absolutely straight line on dry tarmac before putting the pedal to the metal.

It was one of the 427's few reported vices. The new suspension was seen as an almost infinite improvement over the near-rigid leaf-spring set-up, the brakes were even more phenomenal than on the 289, the cockpit was bigger and more comfortable, except for the unfortunate proviso that it did get indescribably hot.

STREET WISE

Once AC had completed the run of competition cars (full racers and what Shelby eventually sold as S/Cs plus three additional chassis), they could start on street-spec 427s.

The street-spec cars had another identity number twist, starting at CSX3101 and therefore leaving a gap after the last of the competition and S/C cars, which had run to CSX3053, plus the three odd chassis: CSX3054, originally intended to be a 427 'Super Coupe' along Daytona lines; CSX3055, which became a Ghia-bodied Willment racing coupe; and CSX3063, which was also given a Ghia body, but as a show car.

Huge sidepipes are typical of a competition spec car.

Brock designed the Sunburst wheels when Halibrand had foundry problems and could not keep up the supply.

The 427 was a beautiful-looking car in road trim, and is nowadays the most coveted Cobra of all.

The road spec 427 is a little less cluttered than the sports car and the narrower wheels look a bit more lost inside the big arches, but the aggression is still there.

It is a bit bigger, but the interior has changed very little in basics from the 289. The rollover-bar is an essential competition extra.

The first three street cars were treated as prototypes, and used to cure remaining problems, notably excessive temperatures both under the bonnet and in the cockpit, the latter using ducting from the two additional holes near the headlights. Other details that were resolved included a more progressive throttle linkage, speedometer recalibration, closed-circuit crankcase breathing, and a new front bumper bar.

It is worth outlining the three basic specs: street, semi-competition and full-race. Street cars usually had two four-barrel Holley carbs on a low-rise manifold, most S/C cars had the medium riser, otherwise the engine specs were very similar, except that S/Cs had the full-race engine's bigger sump, remote oil-filter and oil-cooler. Full-race cars had the high-rise manifold as standard, with the medium riser as an option, usually with a single four-barrel Holley in a cold-air box under the hood-scoop. Race cars had aluminium heads with 12.4:1 compression (compared to the usual 10.4), and they claimed 485bhp (compared to 425).

Street and S/C cars had electric fans ahead of the radiator; full-race cars did not. Street cars had cast-iron exhaust manifolds and exhausts emerging under the back of the car, while S/Cs and racers had tuned tubular manifolds and side pipes; the S/Cs with a degree of silencing, the racer's with none at all. S/C and race cars supplemented the standard mechanical fuel pump with two electric pumps, and had 42-gallon (191-litre) tanks in place of the street car's 18-gallon (81.5-litre) one.

S/C and full-race cars sat on 7.5in (190mm) wheels front and 9.5in (241mm) rear, instead of the street car's 7.5in (190mm) equipment all round and, of course, had appropriate tyre equipment, though still generally from Goodyear.

Road cars had anti-roll bars listed as an option; S/C and race cars had them as standard. S/C and race cars had heavier-duty, quick-change brake calipers, and

3.77:1 final drives as standard, compared to the normal 3.54, although there were obviously numerous options for racing.

Full-competition cars also had the bronze suspension bushes where the others had rubber bushes, and S/C and race cars had even less trim than the road car's already fairly minimal fittings, and neither of them had the road car's glovebox.

Bodywork differed mainly around the wheelarch layouts and cooling and breathing arrangements; like hood scoops and brake-cooling ducts, but varied anyway through the life of the car. S/C and race cars had roll bars and quick-lift jacking points built-in, and the full-race car offered a small racing windscreen.

Even when the specification details were complete, initial production was painfully slow because Shelby was still suffering component supply delays, notably with the special Halibrand magnesium-alloy wheels. After managing for a while by supplying cars on whatever wheels were available, Shelby engineered a longer-term solution by having Pete Brock design a completely new wheel for the 427s, which became known as the 'Sunburst' pattern for its ten spokes radiating from the hub. The one small irony was that Halibrand were the only people who could make it.

WHAT'S IN A CUBIC INCH?

There was a more fundamental spec change, too, early in the life of the 427, when it was decided to give Ford 1966 model-year mainstream production cars the Galaxie 428 engine instead of the original 427. Now one cubic inch might not sound like much of a difference, but the 428 (7,014cc) engine was a totally different breed from the race-bred 427.

In 1966, Ford had withdrawn from NASCAR for most of the year, because their 'ultimate' NASCAR engine, a single-overhead-cam version of the 427 (never offered in the Cobra), had been effectively outlawed. Ford could revert to using the well-proven 427 for racing, but they also introduced a less extreme engine for the road, the 428.

The story is now quite complicated, but worth outlining. First of all, the classic 427 was not actually a 427 at all, it displaced 425cu in (6,964cc). Unfortunately for Ford marketing, Oldsmobile already had a 425 engine in their line-up, so Ford used a bit of poetic licence and named their engine the 427, after the NASCAR limit, equating to seven litres.

That was fine until the milder '428' came along because the 428 genuinely did displace exactly 427cu in (6,997cc)!

Ford marketing did not want to emphasize the differences too much. Officially the classic 427 was the 7-litre Cobra High-Performance V8, and the 428 was the Thunderbird 7-litre Four-Barrel V8, but they were really chalk and cheese. The 'Police Interceptor' 428 was much less over-square than the 427, at 4.13 × 3.98in (104.9 × 101.0mm), it was more simply built, without the main-bearing cross-bolting for instance, and markedly less powerful.

Shelby spec 428s used a single Ford four-

The A.C. 289 sports car has the same basic chassis, suspension and steering specification as the A.C. 428 Convertible, but is 6 ins. shorter in the wheelbase, and is fitted with a 270 bhp high performance 4.7 litre V.8 engine with mechanical tappets, and a manual all synchromesh 4-speed gear box. The new coil sprung suspension and chassis with 4 in. main tubes provide exceptional stability at high speeds with a comfortable ride on secondary roads at touring speeds. The chassis and suspension of the A.C. 289 sports is exactly the same as that used in the construction of the 7-litre Cobra, which is also built at the A.C. Factory, Thames Ditton, and shipped to Shelby American in Los Angeles. Both cars owe their origin to the Mk. 1 Cobra, which for two years running was the winner of the coveted and highly disputed Manufacturers Championship competing with the fastest Works sports car teams from both sides of the Atlantic.

Past A.C. victories include :—
Sports Car Championship of America, 1963, with outright wins too numerous to list during that year.
First British car to finish the Le Mans 24 hour race, 1963.
First in the G.T. Class Le Mans 24 hour race, 1964.
First, Second and Third G.T. Class, 1964, T.T. Race. Goodwood.
Manufacturer's F.I.A. G.T. Championship, 1964 & 1965.

A.C. 289 SPORTS

AC combined the 289 engine with the coil-spring chassis for European consumption, and made one of the best behaved Cobras of all.

Wind deflectors were a token concession to comfort.

The hood never did very much for Cobra's looks.

Round rear lights were a sign of a late model, and one of the very few running changes beyond variations in wheelarch profiles and cooling ducts.

Towards the end of the line.

barrel carburettor and a 10.4:1 compression ratio, to give 390bhp at 5,200rpm and 475lb ft of torque at 3,700rpm in Cobra trim. It was a lot heavier than the specialist 427, too, but the power to weight ratio it gave the Cobra was still a great deal more than almost any street driver had ever had under his foot elsewhere.

One other consideration in adopting the 428 was cost: where a basic 427 cost $730, a 428 cost only $320, which, on a 427 Cobra that listed at only $7,495 for a street car, was a significant sum. A basic competition-spec car typically listed at around $9,500, but it seems likely that 427s generally sold at a loss, probably of around $1,000 a car to the factory.

Shelby did amend his brochures to include the 428 spec, but did not advertise the change any more than Ford did; the Cobra kept its '427' tag, and even now it is virtually impossible to know which cars were fitted with 427s and which with 428s, particularly as, in fact, 427s *were* fitted to some Cobras even after the supposed changeover.

That was one of the very few production changes in the life of the 427. The first fifty-one cars had been to the original 'competition' spec, with wider rear-wing flares, side exhaust cut-outs, and a longish list of other competition options. After that, the cars were mainly street spec, but that was interpreted differently by different owners, given the options available.

The original street bodywork had wide rear-wing flares, but those changed to narrow flares at chassis number CSX3125 and then back to wider ones at 3158 until the end of the run! Rear lights changed from a single rectangular unit (289-style) to two-piece round lights at CSX3201, and the oil-cooler scoop was dropped at chassis number 3301.

Those were pretty well all the changes. In total, Shelby built 260 427 coil-spring street cars, two prototype competition roadsters, nineteen production competition roadsters, thirty-one S/C roadsters, the aborted Daytona 'Super Coupe' and three bare chassis. Add thirty-two COB/COX cars built by AC, and you have a total of 348 coil-spring Cobras.

The last cars were advertised for sale in the USA in August 1968, and the date tells you more or less why the Cobra disappeared when it did. To continue in production in the light of growing environmental protection and safety legislation, the car would have had to change beyond all recognition, and neither Shelby nor Ford were interested in doing that. AC tried briefly, later, with the more refined but hugely less successful Frua-bodied AC428, but ran head-on into the energy crisis of the early 1970s anyway.

Furthermore, Shelby and Ford no longer needed the Cobra for racing, and the simple fact was that it had had its time. So it went out of production, but it never went out of favour, and even now the 427 still ranks as the fastest full production car ever built. Shelby had achieved his dream.

7 The Competition Roadsters

Whatever else the Cobra existed for, it existed for racing. Admittedly, the production roadgoing Cobras were a lot more than coincidental. The vast majority of Cobras *were* roadgoing cars pure and simple, but they were something less than the Cobra's *raison d'être*. You only have to think back to Carroll Shelby and his little team of 1961 to understand that.

Shelby was a racing driver (or at least a recently-retired racing driver); his staff of one, Pete Brock, was a racing driver; his contacts at Ford were racing people; his living was teaching people to drive racing cars, and selling racing tyres to people who could already drive them. He was not a car salesman, not even a sports car salesman; he was a racer through and through and, on top of all that, he wanted to beat Ferrari.

He said almost as much the first time he showed his new car to the press on 10 April 1962, even before it appeared in public at the New York Show three weeks later. When cars began to arrive from England to be completed by Shelby in California, it was only the second series-built car that became the first 'works' racing Cobra.

A VERY VERSATILE RACER

Shelby's ambitions included Europe and Ferrari. A lot of other people had racing ambitions that were not quite so grand as that, but which the Cobra catered for, too. It was not an expensive car, remember – not in relation to its performance – but with its extraordinarily high power-to-weight ratio and its nimble circuit handling, it could blow far more exotic and expensive machinery into the weeds.

And that, for most of its life, was its forte; not as a major-league international racer, although it made its mark there too, but as one of the most prolific winners of all time in such series as the SCCA and USRRC (United States Road Racing Club) Production classes and their European equivalents.

Crowning it all, Shelby finally did beat Ferrari in Europe. He did it in 1965 with the Daytona, a Cobra under its coupe skin, admittedly, and a leaf-spring Cobra at that, but a lot more than a Cobra too, and built only in a series of half a dozen cars.

What might have happened if Shelby had had the 427 homologated as planned for 1965, or if Ford had not complicated the equation with their GT40, or if Shelby had not abandoned the 'Super Coupe' idea, is all a matter for conjecture; what is real enough is that the Cobras and the Daytona did establish a formidable racing record through the 1960s, with nothing much more sophisticated than the old tubular chassis and lots of good, strong Detroit horses.

THE FIRST RACE

It all began in October 1962, appropriately enough right outside Shelby's modest front-door, at Riverside. The car was CSX2002, the second production Cobra; the event was a supporting race for the Riverside GP. It was a race sanctioned by the SCCA who, at a late stage, had added an 'experimental' class, designed largely to give the as yet non-homologated 327 Corvette a chance to show off in public without taking the points from the properly eligible racers. If Chevy could run the Corvette as an experimental car, Shelby was pretty quick to spot a race for his also non-homologated Cobra.

So Billy Krause, a west-coast driver of some repute, with cars including Jaguar D-Types and Maserati Birdcages, and a former winner of the Riverside GP, became the first man to race a Cobra. The car was virtually standard, with 260cu in (4,261cc) engine, and not much more than wider wheels, a long-range fuel tank, a racing windscreen and a tack-on bonnet scoop to distinguish it from any Cobra road car. It carried race number XP98, against the new Corvette's symbolic 00.

Chevrolet's men must have hated it; the Cobra (an idea GM had turned down, remember) simply waltzed away from the Corvette and everything else right from the start of the race, building a lead of 1½ miles

One of the best-known Cobra competition roadsters is the ex-Tommy Atkins, ex-Chequered Flag 289, built in 1964 and typical of a European-spec Cobra racer.

The ex-John Woolfe 427 Semi-Competition started as a prolific British race winner in the mid-1960s and became a magnificent road car, later rebuilt by Brian Angliss' Autokraft.

before succumbing to a broken rear hub (one of the components that had already been strengthened) after about an hour's racing, losing a wheel and spinning into retirement. It was an hour in which Shelby finally learned that he had a potential winner and Chevrolet learned that they had big trouble ahead.

The next outing for the Cobra was at the annual Nassau Speed Week meeting in December 1962, and this time three Cobras were entered. Speed Week was always a festive outing, with a holiday atmosphere,

but Shelby took the racing seriously. The three entries consisted of a full 'works' entry for Krause, a works-built car prepared by ace tuners Holman & Moody for Augie Pabst, and a works-built but privately-owned car for John Everly.

Modifications on the Nassau entries included 12.0:1 compression ratio pistons and roller camshafts, special exhaust manifolds with straight side-exhausts, electric fuel pumps, special ignition systems, bigger sump and an oil cooler. On the chassis side there were stiffer springs and Koni dampers, a 38-gallon (173-litre) fuel tank, alloy brake calipers plus cooling ducts, front and rear anti-roll bars, and a forward-braced roll-hoop. The top of the driver's door was also cut away to give a touch more elbow room, and that later became a common modification where allowed.

This time, Krause was put out by a broken steering mount, which led to a strengthening bracket from Phil Remington for next time out and thoughts of an early change from worm-and-sector to rack-and-pinion. The most successful of the Nassau cars was Everly's, which won one of the five-lap qualifying heats but finished only 16th in its main event.

It might not have sounded like much of a start to a major domestic and international racing career, but the point was that Shelby was learning through experience and modifying the Cobra as he went along. That was how the racing programme would work for some time to come.

Every racing Cobra started life as a road car, and the racers as converted from them fell into three categories, much as at the Nassau race. There were the works cars, the works-prepared/privately entered cars, and the full independents. Of the seventy-three leaf-spring Cobras (from a total of 655, remember) that Shelby American Automobile Club list as having known racing histories, thirty-three were works cars, twelve were works-prepared, and twenty-eight were private entries.

Although there were obviously some basic similarities, there was really no such thing as a standard racing spec in the early days; the cars changed virtually every time out, as either Shelby or one of the other entrants learned something new. First of all, of course, a lot of the effort went into stopping the cars breaking, which generally led to more beefing up in the hubs, the steering and the final-drive mountings. Once the cars would stay in one piece the emphasis switched to making them ever quicker.

TURNING INTO A WINNER

The Cobra's first full race win came in January 1963 at an SCCA Divisional meeting at Riverside, where Shelby had two cars out for Ken Miles and Dave MacDonald. The cars were basically similar to the Nassau ones but with Remington's steering brace, Weber-carburetted engines with a cold-air scoop to feed them, and dual brake master cylinders. It was MacDonald who won the race, with Miles making it a Cobra 1–2.

With commendable marketing opportunism, that led to Shelby advertising the availability of 'Riverside Replica' Cobras, identical to the cars as raced except for the option of Halibrand magnesium wheels instead of the overstressed wire wheels used previously. The cars were offered at $9,000 (plus $500 for the wheel option) but only one car, CSX2017, seems to have been sold as a 'Riverside Replica'.

Most customers seemed happy to formulate their own detailed specifications. What could be done to any car depended first, of course, on what was allowed in the class it would race in.

In SCCA and USRRC production racing, in spite of the name, that was not too different from what was allowed by the FIA's GT rules. Engine components (except for pistons) could be lightened and balanced, and cylinder heads and camshafts modified. Silencing was not required, and side exhausts were permitted. Shelby had homologated a wide range of carburettors, up to and including the exotic four-Weber set-up. Gearbox and final drive ratios could be changed, and the clutch could be modified. Racing tyres could be used, and so could heavy-duty dampers. The main restriction was that overall car weight could not be reduced by more than five per cent; given that the Cobra was already pared to rock-bottom anyway, that was more an advantage than a disadvantage, as it meant that heavier cars were not allowed to catch up. In one respect, the FIA was more restrictive than SCCA or USRRC in requiring a standard windscreen to be fitted, and that seemingly trivial rule was a major drawback for the Cobra roadsters in Europe because the tall, flat screen made the brick-like car's aerodynamics even worse.

Not everybody in the smaller series took advantage of everything allowed, of course, and some cars were a lot closer to stock than others. Typical modifications fell into definite areas: there were safety modifications like roll hoops, competition seat and full-harness belts; there were chassis modifications for better handling and braking, and bigger wheels and tyres to put more power to the ground; and there were such engine modifications as specific rules would allow.

Shelby offered plenty of choices of engine spec. By the time the 289 engine had appeared, standard road tune meant 271bhp. Above that, there was a road/race engine (suitable for street use during the week and some modest competition at the weekend), several levels of full-race engine, and some specialized engines for drag-racing. There was even a specialized car for drag-racing, the Dragonsnake, of which more elsewhere.

The main areas for modification in all the racing engines were the cylinder heads, the camshaft and carburation, and the exhaust manifolding. The road/race engines had mildly modified cylinder heads with bigger valves and matched ports, plus pistons with valve cut-outs to allow higher revs. The full competition heads had big valves and ports, with modified water passages for better cooling, higher compression ratio, stronger, matched valve-springs for more reliable high revs, and rocker pivots threaded rather than pressed into the heads. They were held down with stronger studs and used thin steel-shim racing gaskets. The drag-racing heads were similar but with even bigger valves and ports.

Camshafts and induction were open to a wide range of choices, both from Shelby and from outside tuners. Top-of-the-range carburation was the four 48IDM twin-choke downdraught Weber set-up, which was expensive (at over $1,230 in 1964) but effective.

You could also order special tubular exhaust manifolds (another major power improver), racing distributor, several choices of baffled or large capacity sumps in steel or aluminium (although Shelby themselves never offered a dry-sump option), and an explosion-proof scatter-shield for around the flywheel. Or you could buy the whole thing ready assembled, off the shelf. Also in 1964, a complete road/race engine (less carburettors) was advertised at $729; a full-race engine less carbs at $2,045; and a full-race engine with four Webers for $3,295 – all this at a time when a complete Cobra road car sold for $5,995.

Power varied according to exact specifications and individual engines, of course, but it was possible to have over 360bhp from a heavily modified race engine on a single four-barrel Holley carburettor, or 385bhp (with reliability) for a full-house racing engine with Webers and everything else.

GOING INTERNATIONAL

The latter engines were mainly for the more intense competition of international racing, and once the Cobra was homologated at the end of 1962, that was where Shelby's main interests lay for the next three years.

The Cobra's first international outing was at Daytona in 1963, under FIA Manufacturers' Championship GT class rules, head to head with Ferrari; and it was not just the Cobra's first international outing, it was also the first time that the car would be asked to compete in an endurance race – three hours in this case.

Shelby entered three cars, for Riverside winner Dave MacDonald, Dan Gurney, and

The 'office' of the 289 racer is little different from road cars other than in safety additions such as a roll-hoop, kill-switch and extinguisher bottle.

Wheelarch extensions accommodate extra rubber and cooling slots, and bumpers give way to quick-lift jacking points.

(Right) Engine in ex-Le Mans coupe 39 PH now has single four-barrel Holley in place of four Webers used for racing, and the car is perfectly usable on the road.

(Left) The underbonnet layout of the 289 leaf-spring roadster, even in full competition spec, is straightforward and easily managed.

Skip Hudson. The cars had tack-on wheelarch spats to cover as much tyre as was required by the FIA rules, full wind-screens, which the FIA also required, and Halibrand pin-drive magnesium wheels for strength (the pin-drives proving necessary because the original splines had proved unable to cope with all the torque).

Gurney's car was originally fitted (at Ford's request) with an experimental all-alloy engine, but that had problems immediately before the start of the race. Gurney had to start just as the rest of the field left the grid, after a lightning change back to a normal all-iron engine.

The car did not finish anyway. Like the others, it ran well, but it went out with ignition problems after forty-eight laps, after which Gurney went to work in the pits! Hudson had the potentially more disastrous experience of the flywheel disintegrating and the debris jamming the steering, causing him to spin off. MacDonald, however, having also overcome an electrical problem and a problem in restarting the car after his pit-stop to cure it, survived to finish fourth – behind two Ferrari GTOs and a Corvette.

So reliability was still a problem, and proved to be so again on the Cobra's next international outing, a few weeks later, at the Sebring 12-hour race in March.

There was one road-car-based private entry for Sebring, and five factory cars, with Weber-carburated 289 engines and rack-and-pinion steering for the first time. They also had a lot of minor bodywork modifications over the Daytona cars, new instruments and quick-change front brakes, but were otherwise similar.

It was not a good race for the team. The private entry and two of the works cars failed to finish, and the best of the ones that did was Phil Hill and Ken Miles in 11th place overall and a disappointing eighth in the GT category, with the other two way back in 28th and 38th.

Dan Gurney did give the Cobra its first international level win at Bridgehampton in September 1963, in the FIA-sanctioned Bridgehampton Double 500 endurance race, driving one of the works 'Le Mans Replica' cars, but with a lot of work clearly to be done after Sebring to make the Cobra competitive in FIA company, the works cars were largely delegated to contesting the USRRC championship and selected SCCA Championship rounds for the rest of 1963. They were very successful and, with developing reliability, managed to win the USRRC Manufacturers' title and take first and second places in the Drivers' Championship, for works drivers Bob Holbert and Ken Miles. That was the first year of the USRRC Championship, which was in effect the forerunner of the Can-Am Championships, and open to any closed-wheel sports car, which put the Cobras up against some very specialized racing machinery. The Cobras scored 111 points to Ferrari's 28 and Chevrolet's 19.

In SCCA Production events, the Cobra had started winning regularly at Regional level in southern California, then at Divisional level, and very quickly at National level. In July, Cobras finished 1–2–3 in an SCCA A-Production race at Lake Garnett Raceway, Kansas, and then Ken Miles, by virtue of adding an oil-cooler to his car, put himself into the Modified class and proceeded to run away from even the specialized sports racing cars like the Chaparral and the Cooper-Monaco.

In June 1963, *Road & Track* magazine had said:

It is very hard to imagine that any well-prepared, well-driven Cobra will be beaten this year – not by the Corvettes, and possibly not by anyone . . .

They were very close to being right. The privately-entered Cobras of Bob Johnson and Bob Brown took first and second places in the SCCA A-Production Championship to add to the first of many domestic successes for the Cobras. They went on to win both the

USRRC championship and the SCCA S-Production title again in 1964 with the 289s, and when the 427s took over, they won the SCCA A-Production titles in 1965, 1966, 1967, 1968 and 1973. The 427 might not have had a particularly spectacular international career thanks to the Daytona and the GT40, but it took some beating on home ground.

FIRST TIME TO LE MANS

The 427 was still to come, though. For 1963, Shelby still had the problem of making the 289 work on the world stage and there were obviously times when he knew he was on a loser. Presumably accepting that he did not yet have any chance of being competitive against the best of the Europeans in their most specialized race of all, for example,

Shelby wisely decided not to enter cars at Le Mans in 1963, but to wait until he could do it properly in 1964.

There *were* two Cobras at Le Mans in 1963, though, and they would not be totally disgraced. They would be the first Cobras built specifically as race cars, by AC but on behalf of Shelby. One of them, CS2131 (the missing X indicates that the car was never intended for export), was entered by AC themselves, for English driver Peter Bolton, and Scotsman Ninian Sanderson (who had won Le Mans in 1956, with an Ecurie Ecosse D-Type); the other Cobra, CSX2142, was entered by Shelby's biggest dealer, Ed Hugus of Pittsburgh, for Hugus himself and Englishman Peter Jopp.

Before building the actual Le Mans car, AC built a 'Le Mans prototype' on chassis number CSX2130. This one was completed in April 1963 and delivered to Jopp for race

Le Mans 1963, and 39 PH is on its way to seventh place overall, driven by Ninian Sanderson and Peter Bolton.

This car looks much as the original except for the smaller oil-cooler and different colour scheme.

The car originally had side exhausts, but now runs on the conventional system in deference to road manners.

The large side vents, first incorporated for Le Mans 1963, later passed into road car spec.

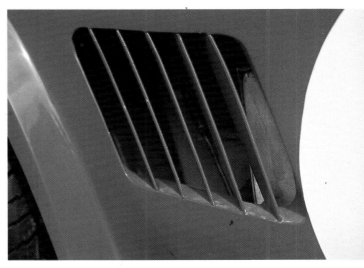

testing. It was the first Cobra with vents in the front wings for additional cooling, and with the 'FIA-type' integral bonnet scoop. It was also a right-hand-drive car. So was CS2131, although CSX2142, designated 'American Le Mans car' in AC's records, was the familiar left-hand drive.

The biggest difference between the prototype and the race cars was that the race cars had gained a new style of hard-top, not the old, short, bubble-style, but a new type that virtually transformed the roadster into a fastback and would clearly help with the aerodynamics on the long Mulsanne Straight.

Shelby supplied Weber-carburetted engines in a relatively mild state of tune, probably around 355bhp, for long-distance reliability, and AC ran them with a 3.31:1 final-drive ratio. That gave a maximum

The Sunday Times *sponsored the 1963 Le Mans effort, which was pit-managed by Stirling Moss. The car was shown off at the newspaper's offices before the race.*

With the improved shape of the special hardtop, the 'coupe' was good for around 167mph (269kph) on the Mulsanne, with only a mild engine tune.

speed of 167mph (269kph) on the Mulsanne, and a best lap of 4 minutes 15.3 seconds, well off the sub-four-minute pace of the quickest qualifiers.

The cars ran on Dunlop alloy centre-lock wheels and wide-section racing tyres that required front and rear wing extensions to satisfy the FIA regulations about covering the tyre treads. They had long-distance 38-gallon (173-litre) fuel tanks and large quick-release filler caps up on the rear edge of the hardtops, which necessitated an extra-short boot-lid.

During practice, Bolton and Sanderson's car lost its rear window at near maximum speed, sucked out by the low pressure behind the car. For the race, the window was held in by supplementary bolts all the way round.

The Hugus/Jopp car retired during the eleventh hour of the race (while running 13th) when a connecting-rod broke, but it was probably just about to be disqualified anyway, for taking on oil before it was permitted to.

It was a race of attrition in which only thirteen cars from the forty-nine starters (which included no less than eleven Ferraris) finished. The Bolton/Sanderson Cobra,

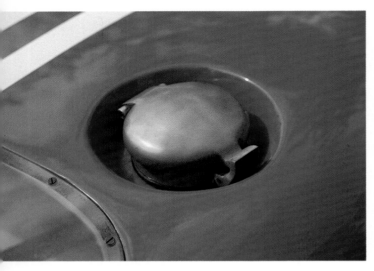

The filler cap was located in the roof, just by the rear window, and connected to the tank by a large pipe.

(Right) The fastback hardtop was an effort to improve aerodynamics and hence top speed on the Mulsanne Straight. It was successful, but the rear window had to be bolted in after air pressure removed it at near maximum speed.

The cockpit of the Le Mans racer was virtually the same as for the standard car.

sponsored by *The Sunday Times* and managed (like the other Cobra) by Stirling Moss, kept rumbling round reliably if unspectacularly, to finish seventh overall (behind six Ferraris!), and fourth in the GT class. It was at least the first car home of the race's three 'British' survivors.

Although the Le Mans effort had not been especially successful, Shelby did commission a short run of 'Le Mans replica' cars for both works and private use, which joined the existing Shelby cars in contesting the rest of the USRRC and SCCA races that year until they were replaced by new FIA/USRRC spec roadsters for 1964, the old team cars being sold off to private entrants. Some private teams did run cars in FIA events too, but with predictably limited success.

1964 – A YEAR OF CHANGES

Also back on home ground, Shelby's next major outing was not until 1964, by which time he had had AC build a new series of five more purpose-built racers, this time specifically for FIA GT competition, where he was still determined to make his mark. The specifications included virtually everything that had been tried and found to work up to that point, plus wider wings to allow for the fitting of wider wheels and tyres as the season went on – and that also involved another driver's door cutback. The cars also had to have a hump moulded into the boot-lid to accommodate the notional 'suitcase' which the FIA deemed all cars should be able to carry.

The first two of the new cars appeared at Daytona in February 1964, for Dan Gurney/Bob Johnson and Jo Schlesser/Jean Guichet. Another Cobra driven by Dave MacDonald with Bob Holbert led by six laps at one point from the pursuing pack of Ferrari GTOs, but was put out of the race by a fire in the pits while refuelling. That, however, was no ordinary Cobra, it was the first of the Daytona coupes whose aerodynamic bodies would eventually help Shelby achieve his aim of beating Ferrari in Europe; but the Daytona merits a chapter of its own (*see* page 157).

All Shelby eventually salvaged out of Daytona 1964 was a fourth place overall (and fourth GT) for Gurney and Johnson. To make it worse for Shelby, they were only beaten by three Ferraris, but now he at least knew that with the Daytona (as the coupe was quickly dubbed after its first outing) he could run with the best of them.

There was another different Cobra out at Sebring in March alongside the usual roadsters, Miles's first attempt at stuffing a 427 engine into a leaf-spring chassis, as already described.

Shelby's 289 roadsters at Sebring had very mixed luck. Gurney and Johnson were entered to drive one car, Bob Bondurant/Lew Spencer a second, and Phil Hill/Jo Schlesser the third. Bondurant and Spencer took fifth place overall and second place in the GT class, with Hill and Schlesser just behind them for sixth/third. Johnson was fortunate to survive a truly huge accident during the night, when he ran over the back of a slow-moving Alfa with no lights on and totally destroyed his roadster.

Shelby was no doubt consoled by the fact that Holbert and MacDonald in the Daytona had taken fourth overall and actually won the GT category ahead of the Ferraris, and Shelby had taken several Ford executives along to watch the race.

Whatever else it meant, it certainly meant that Shelby now knew that if he was going to beat Ferrari at all he was going to do it with a coupe and not a roadster and, from there on, for the works at least, the competition life of the open-top 289s was strictly limited.

It was by no means over, though, and Shelby continued to enter roadsters in FIA races in Europe right through the 1964 season, albeit latterly alongside the Daytonas which were in serious contention for the manufacturers' title.

In many cases they kept earning minor but valuable points towards Shelby's championship tally, but, in some places, they were horribly out of their depth and nowhere more so than around the tortuous island roads of Sicily, in the Targa Florio.

Five roadsters were entered for the 1964 Targa (but no Daytonas), and for a while they actually led, but the rough roads knocked hell out of the old leaf-spring chassis and the only car to be classified was the works entry driven by Gurney and Jerry Grant, in eighth place overall and second in

the GTs. Even that car had broken rear suspension, one other had the same problem, another had a steering breakage and the last had a seized engine caused by a broken oil pipe. For once, Porsches ran away with the glory rather than Ferraris, but this was not a race to remember for Shelby and the Cobras.

Nor, frankly, was much else in 1964 for the roadsters, even though weight of numbers did mean that they won the majority of Shelby's FIA points. At Spa, their best finish was ninth overall and sixth in GT for Bondurant and Jochen Neerspach (later European competitions manager for both Ford and BMW). At the Nurburgring,

After Le Mans, AC's entries had long and successful lives in other European racing. This is the Willment entry at the 1964 Ilford Trophy race at Brands Hatch, won outright by Jack Sears.

The 427 S/C (above and right) was an inspired answer to early problems of shifting stock, but needed considerable skill to master.

Schlesser and Dickie Attwood managed 23rd place overall and sixth again in the GT class.

The big one was next, Le Mans, but Shelby's major effort was naturally in the aerodynamic and now very competitive Daytona coupes, and the roadsters were very much second string. The Daytona obliged with the GT win and fourth overall, while the best of the roadsters was a virtually standard car driven by two French amateur drivers, back in 19th place. Shelby had entered the car largely as a sop to the scrutineers, knowing that if the French car got through, his own really had to, too, and French scrutineers rarely threw out a French entry.

At this point in the 1964 season, Shelby was still well in contention for the FIA GT Championship, but in the end he missed it by 6.3 points, with 78.3 to Ferrari's 84.6.

The scoring system was complicated. Only the first car of any make scored, on a scale of 9–6–4–3–2–1 for the first six places, and the points were multiplied by a coefficient depending on the difficulty of the race.

*Sears in a slightly second-hand looking 289 on his way to fourth place overall
in the 1964 Tourist Trophy at Goodwood.*

In brief, Shelby had a disastrous outing in the Tour de France, which was as much rally as race, and where none of the Daytonas finished. The Cobras did much better in the RAC Tourist Trophy at Goodwood, headed by the Daytona again, but with two roadsters backing up, and then Shelby's hopes of taking the fight for the championship right to the line went up in smoke.

OFF-TRACK CHICANERY

Ironically, given Shelby's reasons for being in the fray in the first place, it was another blatant piece of political chicanery by Ferrari that effectively sealed the 1964 GT Championship.

The final championship round should have been the Monza 1,000km in October, and at one point Shelby could even have had a prototype 427 coupe out there, but in the end the race was cancelled completely after a Ferrari-engineered dispute between the organizers and the FIA over the eligibility of the Ferrari LM. In a nutshell, if Shelby could not win points at Monza, Ferrari could not lose the championship.

Once again, Carroll Shelby was less than impressed by Enzo Ferrari's way of doing

Roger Mac with trouble looming at Goodwood in the 1965 Tourist Trophy, when GPG 4C was being campaigned by The Chequered Flag.

things. His only consolation at the end of a season when he could and probably should have won, was a clean-sweep for his roadsters at the final championship round, at Bridgehampton, though with no chance of making any difference to the result of the championship. The SCCA and USRRC titles were good, but not the same as beating Ferrari.

And that, in effect was the end of the big-league racing career of the Cobra roadsters. The 427 was a very different proposition in 1965 from what the 289 had been in 1963: it was fearsomely quick but still not really the thing for European-style long-circuit racing, and with the works committed to other machinery, such development as was done had to be done by the privateers.

As USRRC racing edged closer to its Can-Am format and domination by big, mid-engined sports racing cars, even Miles could not keep the front-engined 427 roadster in contention. Even in SCCA racing, the 427 never appeared in the same numbers as the 289s had, but the 427s that did race did so with devastating effect, as those five additional SCCA A-Production titles from 1965 to 1973 show. One of the first 427 owners, Hal Keck, won in 1965; Ed Lowther won in 1966; and Sam Feinstein was the shock winner several years after it looked as though the 427 had won its last, with that 1973 title, actually gained with Lowther's old car.

There were occasional international outings for 427s, too, but only to individual races, never any concerted championship effort. Most of the entries were in US-based rounds of the FIA Championships, like

Daytona and Sebring, but even drivers like Keck and Lowther could not achieve anything at that level. In Europe, Tony Settember and Ed Feutel campaigned a 427 in several events, usually without finishing. The 427's best ever European result was an outright win for Bob Bondurant and David Piper in the Ilford Trophy race at Brands Hatch in 1966 against good opposition.

The 427 roadsters were not much of a swansong for the original Cobra concept in racing but, at least with the Daytona, Shelby had found a better way to attack Ferrari properly.

8 The Daytona Coupe

To any outsider, the almost instant success of the Cobra roadster in national racing, and to a lesser degree in international events, must have seemed a major achievement. And it was, but for Carroll Shelby and his team, it was not quite enough.

From the start, Shelby's sights had been on the highest level of international success, and that would stop at nothing short of beating Ferrari, dominant for the last decade, in Europe. But with the leaf-spring 289 Roadsters, Shelby had a problem: the cars were capable of romping away with any kind of sprint race on a twisty circuit with limited straights, using their prodigious power-to-weight ratio to devastating effect, but on the longer straights of a typical European international circuit, they just were not quick enough.

The problem was a fundamental one. Power-to-weight ratio, given adequate traction and properly-chosen gearing, gives acceleration; essentially, the more power and the less weight, the quicker the car will be off the line, or out of the corners. The Cobra had that equation down to a fine art: it had excellent power from its Ford V8 and was carrying no excess weight whatsoever. On a dragstrip, no other production-based racing car would even look at it.

Maximum speed, on the other hand, is governed less by the relationship between power and weight than by the relationship between power and aerodynamic drag. And without being too rude about it, although the Cobra roadster was stunningly handsome, it was about as aerodynamic as the side of a house.

Adding more power was not the answer. For one thing, it simply was not possible to drag more than a few more bhp out of the 289 engine, and with a law of rapidly diminishing returns for horsepower against speed as speed increases, Shelby was looking at the need for *lots* more power to make a roadster usefully quicker.

The prototype 427 that Miles was working on by the beginning of 1964 showed that even adding massive doses of power and torque did not help, not if the car grew more body and cooling drag, and more drag from bigger tyres. The 427 would prove to be ridiculously quick in terms of acceleration, but still not quick enough on the longest of straights.

However, the not especially powerful 289 roadster-based cars that AC and Ed Hugus had run at Le Mans in 1963 had proved capable of a previously unheard of 167mph (269kph) down the three-mile-long Mulsanne Straight, almost entirely on the strength of using new 'fastback' hardtops. Even in the days of the Ace, the Aceca coupe had always been substantially quicker than the roadster with similar engine.

SCIENCE TO THE RESCUE

Aerodynamics were obviously the key, and Shelby knew that if he was to have any serious chance of challenging Ferrari et al. on the international level, he had to have a coupe to do it with. Even while Shelby was thinking about that, Pete Brock, having seen the effectiveness of the AC Le Mans cars, was obviously thinking along the same lines, and so was development engineer cum competitions director Ken Miles.

The front runners at the start of the 1964 race show why Shelby had to do something more scientific than just add horsepower if he wanted to stay in the European racing game. The leading Ferrari is mid-engined and highly aerodynamic, and back on the left of the pack, number 11, is the first of Ford's GT40s. The Daytonas are numbers 5 and 6, here chasing the front-engined Aston and Iso in second and third places.

At Shelby in 1963, that was more or less all it took to get a project under way. This time, too, there was to be another powerful incentive, in that Ford, having watched Shelby and the Cobras' progress to date, clearly thought that a bit of direct financial support could earn a lot of kudos for Ford in 1964. Don Frey eventually suggested around October 1963 that Ford could back Shelby's European efforts reasonably handsomely for 1964.

By that time, Shelby, Brock and team were already scribbling. They knew they wanted a coupe, and they might have liked a few other things besides, like more power and a better chassis, but they only had a matter of months before the season started, and the FIA rules only allowed them a certain amount of leeway, so they just had to do what they could on the old-familiar existing base: the leaf-spring 289 chassis.

They also knew that if it was going to happen in time, they had to do it themselves, there was no point asking Ford or AC or even any outside carrozzeria to get involved in the design process.

The idea was not quite universally accepted at Shelby. Phil Remington, whose main concern was the engines, but who had had only limited experience of specialized European requirements, still believed the goal could be achieved with power, but he was willing to put his bit into developing the coupe anyway.

He also provided someone from his side of the operation who did have a lot more experience of European racing and European regulations. He was one John Olsen, New Zealand-born but who had been working with racing teams in Europe since the late 1950s, including a spell with Bruce McLaren before he joined Shelby. Olsen helped significantly in formulating the overall philosophy of the coupe.

TAKING SHAPE

The project started to take some physical shape around November 1963. Given the name that the car eventually acquired, it might be seen as appropriate that Brock and Miles started work around the remains of the roadster that Skip Hudson had wrecked early in 1963 at Daytona.

The beginnings were very Heath Robinson. Brock took what was left of the bare rolling chassis of CSX2008, laid a hefty piece of corrugated cardboard on the outriggers as a floor to support a very basic glassfibre seat shell, which he moved as low and as far back as was physically possible. He also welded a short length of steering column, with wheel attached, to a small tube attached to the chassis.

Miles, inappropriately dressed in striped jacket and collar and tie, was put into the seat and juggled the steering wheel to a position that was comfortable enough for him as a driver, low enough for Brock as an aerodynamicist. Brock then made up a wooden 'gallows' arrangement to pass over Miles's head to measure the lowest possible position for a roofline.

A photograph of Miles sitting in the 'car', with Brock supporting his measuring square an inch or so above his head, and a shirt-sleeved Shelby standing alongside, shows all three laughing like a bunch of schoolboys doing something silly. It did not turn out to be so silly in the end.

Miles now took responsibility for the chassis, and Brock for the shell. Whether or not at this point they were really expecting the car to be homologated as nothing more than a special-bodied Cobra roadster and allowed to run in the GT class, they worked without imposing too many restrictions other than the ones already inherent in using the existing chassis and running-gear.

The relevant FIA regulations did say that it was permissible to build special bodies onto already homologated chassis without taking them out of the GT class, but they did not really mean to say that the car could be substantially redesigned under the skin, too.

Had the FIA not accepted the Cobra coupe as just a bodywork variation on the roadster, Shelby would have been in real trouble: that would have meant either running in the prototype class or having to build 100 cars in a year to homologate back into the GT ranks. The former would have made the coupe uncompetitive, however much better than the roadster it turned out to be, against more sophisticated, mid-engined opposition; the latter would have been impossible to achieve given the lack of time and resources.

INSTANT ACCEPTANCE

Fortunately for all concerned, and perhaps a little surprisingly, too, the FIA chose to interpret Miles's chassis superstructure as being there only to support the new body, and they homologated the coupe for the GT class without any further argument.

Pete Brock (born 1937)

Carroll Shelby found his first real employee virtually by accident through a friend and fellow racing man of some repute in California, Max Balchowski. Shelby happened to be in Balchowski's racing shop one day and Balchowski told him about a young man looking for a job. The young man was Pete Brock.

Brock was born in New York, in 1937, but brought up and educated in San Francisco. He studied car styling at the Los Angeles College of Design and went to General Motors around 1958 to continue his training as a stylist. He worked on what became the Sting Ray, and also on a project of his own: a small, fastback sports car designed to sell very cheaply. He was allowed to build a full-size styling prototype (with no mechanical parts, of course), which was codenamed Cadet. The chairman called to see it one day, said he did not like small cars, and that was the last that was seen of it, except that some people saw shades of it in the later Corvair. By then, Brock had left GM, as frustrated by the big company slowness as Shelby was around the same time when he was trying to sell them the idea of a European-type sports car with a US V8 engine . . .

Brock went back to California and carried on with his amateur racing career, first with a Cooper, then with various Lotuses, and that brought him into contact first with Balchowski and then with Shelby. Shelby liked the amiable, articulate and obviously talented Brock and took him on as his second employee (the first was the telephonist).

Brock's first role was to get the racing school up and running, which meant everything from administration to preparing the cars to actually teaching. In September 1964, *Car and Driver* magazine described Brock as 'in charge of special projects for Shelby, which seems to include everything from designing letterheads to teaching at the school, designing show-cars to art-directing advertising campaigns . . .' Brock did design everything from the Cobra logos to T-shirts and posters, and inevitably he was involved with the racing side of the Cobra programme, too. He stayed involved with the school until John Timanus took over and allowed him to go to the new Shelby works and start developing the Daytona.

As chief designer, he was involved in all sorts of projects for Shelby. At one point, he was sent to Italy to work with Shelby's old friend Alessandro de Tomaso on a planned mid-engined Shelby racer. The car was part-built when he arrived, but put together so badly that he took it away from De Tomaso and Ghia and had it completed by another coachbuilder. When it was finished, De Tomaso announced it as the Ghia-De Tomaso, as built for Shelby. Shelby, unable for once to obtain backing from Ford, did not take the project up. De Tomaso did, and sent it to Giugiaro, who transformed it into the Mangusta. Mangusta is the Italian for mongoose, and as everyone knows, the mongoose is the deadly enemy of the snake. And the Mangusta eventually gave rise to the mid-engined De Tomaso Pantera – backed initially by Ford!

Brock left Shelby late in 1966, by which time the organization had started to change quite dramatically from the one that he had joined to do everything except answer the telephone. It was a big company by that time, in effect Ford's racing research facility, and getting a bit too close to the corporate mentality for Brock to feel totally comfortable any more. His own projects, notably the 427 Super Coupe, had been overtaken by the need to get the GT40 right, and to develop the MkII, and he was ready for something different.

Something different turned out not to be all that different, but was for Brock himself. He set up Brock Racing Enterprises and got heavily involved in SCCA Production racing with a string of Japanese cars. He started with a team of Hino Contessas, then moved onto Datsuns when Hino were absorbed by Toyota. Shelby was involved with Toyota at that time, with a development contract to race their 2000GTs, and Brock thought the Datsuns (reportedly with a huge racing budget from the company) would give him a chance to have some fun against his old boss.

He ran Datsun 2000 roadsters, 240Zs, and Trans-Am 510 saloons, and the BRE Datsuns won two SCCA C Production National Championships at Road Atlanta in 1970 and 1971.

By the early 1980s he had a successful company building hang gliders. Today, he is director of design and engineering at Kaminari, a company that markets aerodynamic body parts for all kinds of cars. He has not lost touch with Shelby, either: one of Brock's first projects for the 1990s was to help design the Dodge V6-powered Shelby Can-Am racer, as commissioned by the SCCA, and he is still on the advisory board of the Shelby American Automobile Club.

There is very little doubt about the revised chassis' real purpose, of course. The old Ace-type ladder, after all, was never over-endowed with torsional rigidity. The opposition started to rumble with discontent when the coupe showed its potential, but by then all the FIA could do was to keep a very strict eye on the cars at every race, often giving Shelby a hard time about complying, to the letter, with what was homologated on the cars and what was not.

Shelby did not mind that, and even if he had been mildly surprised at how readily the Daytona was accepted by the FIA, he was not about to feel bad about the coupe's rather liberal interpretations of the rules; that, after all, was how Ferrari had turned the fairly mundane 250GTB into the world-beating GTO.

Miles's coupe chassis was a major improvement. A fully-triangulated frame rose from the original large-diameter tubes, completely flanking the engine and transmission to form what was in effect a very strong, light, tubular backbone. A pyramid of tubes continued from the frame which now surrounded the gearbox, to an apex on the new dashboard hoop. Another strong, triangulated hoop behind the driver was chassis strengthening, roll-hoop and body support, all in one. It is a simple but classic piece of spaceframe design, entirely formed from straight tubing and with obviously efficient triangulation.

Brock, meanwhile, was outlining the body shell. He had started with endless sketches, which he taped all round the workshop walls and gradually distilled to one integrated design. He then made a series of finished working drawings. From them he needed to make a body buck on which to form the sheet aluminium panels for the shell.

He did that in the traditional way, building a complete outline of the car in a honeycomb of plywood panels. With very few of the more modern design facilities to hand, Brock transferred the designs from two dimensions to three by photographing his quarter-scale working drawings (showing profiles of the car in all directions through dozens of sections), and then projecting the transparencies to full size, directly onto sheets of plywood propped against the workshop wall. The outlines were drawn from the projected images, the pieces cut and finished, and assembled as a full-scale three-dimensional jigsaw of the car's outline, around which the aluminium panels could be hand-formed and fitted.

For the first car, that was entrusted to the California Metal Shaping company, who also followed the traditional methods: hand-beating individual panels, large and small, and then butt-welding and buffing them together into a single large shell.

THE AERODYNAMICS DEBATE

Brock's coupe outline looked good. It had a much lower nose line than the roadster's, made possible by tilting the radiator steeply forwards and building it into a clever piece of ducting of its own, on Olsen's suggestion, to dump its hot air directly out over the bonnet rather than into the engine compartment. That also, coincidentally, gave a degree of downforce on the front. The nose was longer, with a much smaller air-intake, and the headlights were neatly fared in. There were also additional driving lights let into the nose, flanking the grille opening.

The carburettors on the familiar 289 full-race engine would also be isolated from the engine compartment in their own box, breathing cooler air directly through a hole in the bonnet. The side-exhausts were neatly recessed into the sills below the doors, further to smooth the airflow. The filler cap and air-jack connectors were recessed into the shell, and the coupe ended in a classic, square-chopped, Kamm-type tail.

Brock and crew had considered some kind

of rear spoiler – even including a Porsche 959-like hooped device on some of the earliest drawings – but decided to run the tail unadorned. It was a near thing, though. In *Sports Car International* magazine in May 1990, Brock admitted:

I was trying to keep the Cobra coupe's roof curvature within a seven-degree slope, to minimize airflow separation, drag and lift. Nevertheless, I felt the new coupe would lift at the rear, so I wanted to use a ring-shaped aerofoil similar to what Posche adopted 20 years later on the 959. Shop politics were against such a radical feature and there was neither time nor money available to experiment, so my ring aerofoil idea was never tried on the Cobra coupe . . .

In the end, he did find it necessary to add a simple duck-tail spoiler at the back to negate a worrying high-speed tail-lift, and he did add some detail tweaks that Ford's aerodynamicists, led by Herb Karsh, had suggested. There was a small lip ahead of the radiator exhaust vent, for instance, to create a low-pressure area above the vent and help extract the hot air, and the vent soon lost its original splitter, which restricted airflow slightly. For some circuits, vertical slots were opened up in the outer edges of the concave Kamm tail, for better rear-end cooling, and for others they were covered up.

Brock was very happy to accept advice on such fine-tuning details, but he did not compromise on many things. He stuck by the rather bulbous windscreen and roofline that he had originally conceived, for instance, even in the face of some quite compelling scepticism.

Such scepticism came from another visiting aerodynamicist, Benny Howard, who Shelby had invited along to see the car while it was taking shape on the plywood body bucks. Brock had never claimed to have any formal training as an aerodynamicist, and not even much practical experience beyond what he had done in his brief stint at GM on the Sting Ray project and at Shelby with the Cobras, but he was obviously of the intuitive school and he believed in his design. Howard, with an illustrious background in aircraft design (racing planes as well as highly successful commercial ones), looked at the developing shape, talked to Brock about the roof angle in particular, made a few quick calculations, and suggested to Shelby that even to get it to 160mph (257kph) would take at least 450bhp.

Given that even 400bhp was definitely not possible from a reliable 289 engine and that the fastback hard-topped roadsters at Le Mans in 1963 had already achieved 167mph (269kph) on the Mulsanne with no more than probably 350bhp, that was not something Shelby wanted to hear.

After talking more about the coupe with Howard over lunch, Shelby, obviously worried for once, went and asked Brock what he thought. Brock asked Shelby if he had ever let him down so far; Shelby had to admit that he had not, and Brock's design continued unchanged. True democracy.

Whether Howard could have wrung even more out of the coupe is a matter for conjecture, but it seems highly unlikely. The fact was that, in the end, Brock's design actually worked.

SOME COBRA UNDER THE SKIN

Under the skin, it would have few further changes from the roadsters. The preferred engine used Weber 48IDAs, a lowish compression ratio, typically at around 11.5:1 for variable fuel quality at European circuits, big-valve heads and cams matched for a lot of high speed running. A typical engine would give some 380bhp.

The four-speed Borg-Warner T10 transmission was retained, with closer ratios, and something like a 3.09:1 final drive for the longest circuits, which gave a theoretical maximum of close to 200mph (322kph). The Daytona never actually did that, but it was a good 20mph (32kph) quicker than a roadster with similar power.

It used the same Girling disc brakes all round that were used on the GT40s and the later 427s, and had anti-roll bars as standard, front and rear. There was a lot more underbonnet space than on the roadster, and with better accessibility because the whole nose tilted (plus a small flip-up cover so that oil could be added without lifting the whole nose, and the Daytona took around 2.5 gallons (11.5 litres). It also used a quick-fill radiator system and a long-range, 37-gallon (168-litre) fuel tank. The packaging was tight enough for the steering column to have to thread its way through the exhaust manifold on the driver's side.

The car ran for the first time on 1 February 1964 – at Riverside, of course. Miles was driving, and within a few laps Shelby's men knew that the coupe was dramatically quicker than any roadster. At around 165mph (265kph) on the relatively short Riverside straight, it would have been maybe 10mph (16kph) slower than one of Ferrari's GTOs, but the coupe, which weighed very little more than the roadster, maintained the Cobra's traditional advantage of blistering acceleration.

With its stiffer chassis, and marginally better weight distribution at almost precisely 50/50 front/rear, it handled even better than the roadsters. Unexpected bonuses for Shelby were that the Daytona also showed something close to a 25 per cent improvement in fuel consumption over the roadster, it was more stable at speed, and the brakes ran cooler, all of which would be very useful in long-distance races.

INTO ACTION

There was not much time to do any more testing with the new Cobra coupe, as it was still called in-house, before it had to face the real thing. Its first race was the Daytona Continental, on 12 February 1964, only eleven days after it had first turned a wheel.

Dave MacDonald and Bob Holbert were entrusted with the maiden outing, and the car was going better than anyone could have dared to hope. Eight hours into the race it had a comfortable lead over the Ferrari GTOs, and a new lap record to its credit.

Then Holbert began to have problems with an overheating differential and came into the pits. Olsen rolled under the back of the car to try to find the problem, while the pit-crew put fuel in directly above him. The problem was nothing more serious than the failure of the small electric pump that transferred oil from the diff to its rear-mounted oil cooler, but while Olsen was still under the car, fuel blew out of the tank vents, poured over onto the hot diff casing and immediately turned the back of the car into a ball of flame, with Olsen in the middle.

One quick-thinking crew-member grabbed Olsen's ankles and dragged him, badly burned, from under the car, while others managed to extinguish the fire. The damage was not particularly serious, but it was enough to put the sole Cobra coupe out of the race and rob it of what had looked like a certain debut win. It did not have to wait very long to make amends, only until the next FIA round, in fact, at the Sebring 12-hour race on 27 March.

In the meantime, the car had been repaired and undergone further testing, and Olsen had recovered. Some of the testing was done at Riverside in March, alongside Miles's early testing of his 427 prototype. It included some air-flow testing with the bodywork covered with short tufts of wool, and Dave Friedman riding alongside at high speed in the passenger seat of a 289 roadster, taking photographs of how the tufts were behaving. Shelby did not have a wind-tunnel.

The 427 Super Coupe

Given the success of the aerodynamically superior Daytona in overcoming the 289 roadster's shortage of straightline speed, a coupe-bodied 427 Cobra, with much improved coil-spring chassis, should have been the ultimate Cobra racing weapon.

Everyone involved with the Cobra undoubtedly knew that, and for a while it seemed that there would indeed be a 427-based 'Super Coupe'. In the end, though, the planned car was a victim of Shelby and Ford's clashes of interests, and of some rather sub-standard English workmanship, even before it was properly completed.

Brock started to outline such a car late in 1964, although it had been made clear that he was working to a strictly limited budget because the GT40 was now in the equation too, and Ford were not likely to back both cars. And according to Brock's thinking, they would have been pretty well head-to-head competitors: the Ford making up for its relative lack of power by mid-engined sophistication; the front-engined 427 coupe making up for its relative lack of sophistication with sledgehammer power. Brock was looking for some 215mph (346kph) from his Super Coupe on the Mulsanne Straight at Le Mans, and he was working towards outright wins, not just class wins.

It was not quite his first attempt at a 427 coupe. That had been the car in the middle of the Daytona series, based on chassis CSX2601. In 1964, that chassis had been sent to Italy to be enlarged into a 427-engined leaf-spring Daytona, and it had been completed, bar adding the engine, when its sister Daytona, CSX2300, was damaged in its transporter accident en route to the Tour de France. Thereafter, CSX2601 was reinstated to 289 status and Brock went back to the drawing board to work around the new coil-spring chassis.

At that point, he expected to have the car built as the Daytonas had been, mechanically completed in the USA then shipped to Italy for the best coachbuilders in the business to clothe in a hand-formed aluminium shell. But someone from Ford had a better idea.

That was Peyton Cramer, a young accountant who Ford had given to Shelby around 1964 as 'general manager'. Cramer's job was mainly to get some formal organization into the Cobra build and sales programmes over and above the rather make-it-up-as-you-go-along scheme of things from the early days. He also helped with setting up and controlling the dealer network, and generally with looking after Ford's investment.

He did the same in the early days of the GT40, too, and that was how he came to be at British coachbuilders Harold Radford, in north-west London early in 1965. Radfords were well known for their specialist Mini conversions, for repairs on Rolls-Royces and Bentleys, and for design and development for motor industry customers. One of those customers was Ford, for whom Radford were finishing GT40 interiors. Cramer had called to see them to find out why the work was costing so much.

He also happened to mention the 427 coupe project and Radford responded by offering to take that on for a knock-down price, around $3,000, so long as they kept the GT40 contract too. Cramer told Shelby of the offer and Brock, probably realizing that the car was not going to be built any other way, reluctantly agreed to let Radfords do the job. The working drawings, plus Brock's quarter-scale clay model, were sent to Radford, along with chassis number CSX3054, which was completed by AC as a chassis only, early in 1965.

In theory, Radfords had little else to interfere with the project, but they still had to find additional specialist staff to work on it. In Italy, that would have been the end of the matter until the car was delivered, probably within a couple of weeks; in England it was the beginning of the end for the Super Coupe.

For a while, Radford kept sending progress reports and even though it all seemed to be happening very slowly, Brock stayed at a distance. Then, however, one of Shelby's racing people, in Britain on business, happened to call in on Radford and see what was actually happening. The answer was, not very much – and what *had* been done was a bit of a disaster.

He phoned Shelby, and Brock was soon on his way to see what could be done. He found that Radfords had used totally wrong materials in several places, that the car bore little resemblance to his drawings, that it was bigger, heavier, and really very poorly built.

His first instinct was to bail out of the project altogether because the season was by now well underway anyway and there seemed little hope of getting the car built properly in the immediate future. Ford, however, now became the coupe's ally, because the GT40 programme was not progressing as it ought and the powerful 427 could still save the day for them at a pinch.

They put further pressure on Radfords by threatening to take away the GT40 work, and laid down some new ground rules about schedules and build quality. Radford accordingly promised to find better people and finish the job within a few weeks, with Brock staying on to supervise.

The problem now was that any racing fabricator who was any good was already working for someone else by this stage of the season, so Radford again got the second string. Brock stuck it out for almost another three months (by which time the project was also maybe five times over budget), and then asked for the car to be pulled out of Radfords altogether and taken back to the USA for completion.

Unfortunately for the Super Coupe, by that time Ford had Shelby working on the GT40 project (with Carroll Shelby's one-time benefactor John Wyer, late of Aston Martin, now of Ford Advanced Vehicles also involved), and they were making it work. The one incomplete Super Coupe was therefore shipped back from Radford to Shelby and then more or less abandoned.

It passed through several owners in the late 1960s and the 1970s until it was bought by Craig Sutherland, who eventually had it completed in 1980 by respected fabricator Mike Dopudja of Engelwood, Colorado, with a lot of help from Peter Brock who confirmed how he had really envisaged the car in the first place.

It looks a lot bigger than the Daytonas, not quite so clean limbed, but certainly purposeful. It has an odd nose treatment with two rectangular driving lights in the centre above the air-intake, and it has a distinctive recessed rear window treatment above a steeply sloping Kamm tail with two massive fuel fillers and a large air-slot. It is a right-hand-drive car, with a transparent panel along the front of the roof, both, apparently, to cater for visibility on the high Daytona banking.

How it would have fared against the GT40s will always be a matter for conjecture, but the bad timing meant the only racing that the potentially awesome Super Coupe has ever done has been in the gentler reaches of historic sports car events through the 1980s.

One thing that the earliest tests had shown was that the rear quarter-windows, built out from the bodywork supposedly as scoops to pick up air for rear brake cooling, were actually throwing air out rather than taking it in. What was happening was that air flowing over the body was separating from the car's sides by a couple of inches, leaving a low-pressure area by the windows, and the rear tyres were pumping the air from under the body out of the holes, just by their rotation. That one was solved by adding some small deflectors ahead of the windows to get the air to go in, as planned.

The Daytona always did have a problem, though, of excessive cockpit heat, even when efforts were made to provide more ventilation for the drivers. The cockpit itself was finished in matt-black paint, with virtually no trim whatsoever, and it tended to be like an oven. Some crude vents were hacked into the dashboard, with scoops on the front wings and bulkhead to feed them, but they were only ever a partial solution.

WINNERS' CIRCLE

At Sebring, on 21 March 1964, all the work on the Daytona (as it had inevitably come to be called after its debut outing) paid off. Not only did Holbert and MacDonald comfortably win the GT category in the Sebring 12-hour race, and take fourth place overall, but they were also followed home by three Cobra roadsters, to make a fine day for Ford. They had beaten both Ferrari and the best of the Grand Sport Corvettes.

Having proved the Daytona capable of winning a race, Shelby now had to prove it capable of winning the championship, and he was not going to be able to do that with the single car that had been completed to date, so a Daytona 'production' programme had been started.

It would only ever extend to six cars in total – all of which, incidentally, still exist – but even that was too much for Shelby to tackle without outside help. The bodywork was the main problem, and that was farmed out to the traditional home of the specialist racing body builder, Italy.

On the advice of Alessandro de Tomaso (the car builder, a close friend of Shelby's, and one of the people he had approached first with the Cobra idea), Shelby chose Carrozzeria Grand Sport, in Modena. The first target was to complete another Daytona for Le Mans.

The Italians had the car ready in time for the Le Mans test days, but it was not quite the same as the first car. Somehow the chassis had been delivered to Italy with a body hoop that was a couple of inches taller than it was supposed to be. The Italians, who were quite used to working directly with what they were given, often without proper drawings, assumed it was a legitimate modification and built the car around it, with a taller roofline. In the end, it was a convenient mistake: the taller roof made space in the cockpit for lanky Californian Dan Gurney, who had trouble fitting into the original Daytona at all, and so chassis CSX2299 became 'his' car.

While the second car was being completed, the first, on chassis CSX2287, had made its European debut on 17 May in the Spa 500km race. Shelby had not even taken the Daytona to the Targa Florio, which was hard enough even on the roadsters, but the ultra-fast Spa circuit with its long Masta Straight should have been a perfect circuit for the Daytona.

It should also have been useful preparation for Le Mans, but in the event it proved to be a bit of a disaster. Phil Hill drove the singleton coupe, but spent almost as much time in the pits as on the circuit, cleaning clogged fuel filters presumably caused by locally supplied petrol – a problem that often used to affect racing teams in Europe, even at Le Mans.

All Hill had to show for his efforts at the end of the day was a new GT lap-record, at almost 130mph (209kph), but Ferrari had taken the all-important GT points. Hill had noticed, however, that at very high speeds the tail of the car was getting frighteningly light, and that was the origin of Brock's simple, ducktail spoiler, which would be even more important at Le Mans.

Shelby did not take the Daytona to the Nurburgring 1,000km in 1964, either. The GT40 made its debut there, but Shelby was busy anyway preparing for Le Mans.

WINNING AT LE MANS

The preparation paid off. Both cars made it to Le Mans in June, crewed by Gurney/Bondurant and Chris Amon/Jochen Neerspach. The cars ran well on the pace right from the start, with Amon and Neerspach working their way up to fourth place before falling foul of the regulations. After a routine pit-stop, their car would not start on the button, one of the pit-crew used an auxiliary battery to get it going, and the car was disqualified. It was the penalty Shelby had to pay for how closely the FIA was watching the Daytona after allowing it its homologation.

During the night, Gurney and Bondurant had problems of their own with a broken oil-cooler, falling oil-pressure and an overheating engine, but they nursed the car to the finish while the nearest Ferrari GTO nibbled at their long early lead. The Daytona held on to win the GT class, and to finish an amazing fourth overall – the best a GT car had ever done at Le Mans up to that time, and beaten only by three Ferrari prototypes after the new Ford GT40s had failed.

The Daytona had proved capable of over 180mph (289kph) on the Mulsanne Straight, and had averaged over 117mph (188kph) for the twenty-four hours.

They were now in with a serious chance of taking the GT Championship, which made the next race, at another of the faster European circuits, Reims, very important. The cars stayed in France between events and were completely overhauled in Ford France's workshops, but the Reims 12-hour race on 5 July was not the Daytona's day. Gurney and Bondurant's car retired within the first hour with broken gearbox mounts, and Ireland and Neerspach, who had already lost time with a broken exhaust, succumbed to the same gearbox-mount problem at half distance.

With the number of races now running out, the championship was in the balance. The next time out for the Daytona tipped it Shelby's way as Gurney, against all the odds on a tight circuit that really did not suit the coupes, took another GT class win (and an amazing third place overall) on 29 August at the RAC Tourist Trophy at Goodwood. Phil Hill was the unlucky one again, and spent a lot of time in the pits with the other Daytona having a broken oil line repaired, which relegated him to an 11th place finish.

In theory, that left three events to decide the championship: one that most definitely would not suit the Daytonas, the Tour de France in September; one that would, the ultra-fast Monza 1,000km, scheduled for October; plus the final round on home ground at Bridgehampton.

The Tour de France was a unique event, a near-4,000-mile (6,436km) mixture of eight races and eight hillclimbs, all joined together by open-road sections with very difficult average speed requirements, taking the competitors all across France over a period of more than a week. Two Daytonas were entered, for Bondurant and Neerspach and for French drivers Maurice Trintignant and Bernard Saint-Auban. There should have been a third, but a catastrophic sequence of events rendered it a non-starter.

In fact three more coupes were now under construction. Shelby was going to give it his best possible shot at Monza, of course, and one was to be something special for next year: a heavily modified Daytona with a 427 engine shoehorned in. That car was virtually completed, and the other 289s were not, when the third of the normal coupes, en route for the Tour de France, was badly damaged in a transporter accident. The 427-engined car, already in Italy where it had been bodied as usual at Grand Sport, was hastily converted back to 289 spec, so that Shelby could still have three Daytonas at Monza.

And, after all that, Monza was cancelled anyway, after Ferrari's well-timed protest about the non-homologation of his 250LM as a 'production' car and the skilfully managed showdown between Ferrari, the FIA and the Monza organizers. The FIA refused to accept the LM even when Ferrari threatened to withdraw completely from competition if they did not, but the Monza organizers conveniently averted the inevitable showdown by cancelling their race anyway. Monza, after all, is only a few miles down the road from Maranello.

Shelby was again left to draw his own conclusions about Ferrari, and about whether the race would have been cancelled had it been anywhere else in the world, but unfortunately it was the end of his championship chances for 1964.

The Daytonas had had a disastrous time in the Tour de France, with both cars winning races in the early stages, but then both retiring as the team, with no experience of this sort of event, could not keep them running within the allotted service times. Ferrari cleaned up, of course, and with Monza cancelled, the championship was his.

Shelby did not even take the Daytonas to the final round at Bridgehampton and, in spite of taking all the points with the roadsters, had to settle for missing the title in 1964 by just 6.3 points, with 78.3 to 84.6 for Ferrari.

1965 – SWEET REVENGE

Life was becoming complicated for Shelby by 1965, with the GT40s now occupying all of Ford's and a lot of his attention, and the 427 roadster story starting to unfold. Ferrari's Monza manipulations, though, had made him all the more determined to beat him in the end, and that still had to mean with the Daytona. There should also have been another 427 coupe for 1965, but more of that elsewhere. By the start of 1965, five Daytonas were completed and the sixth was well on its way.

Shelby used them to devastating effect, taking six GT wins and two second places from eight starts, and fielding as many as five of the six cars on one occasion – at Le Mans, of course.

There was perhaps a minor disappointment for Shelby in that Ferrari pulled out of the GT Championship in mid-May in protest at the FIA refusing to homologate his new 275GTB, even though he had built more than 100 by then. It was not too much of a disappointment, though, as Shelby and his Daytona finally *had* whipped Ferrari, with devastating thoroughness in the first three races of the year before he announced his temporary retirement.

At Daytona in February, and Sebring in March, the Daytonas twice finished 1–2–3

in the GT category; at Sebring they even took 1–2–3–4. At Daytona they took second, fourth and sixth overall, led home by Schlesser and Harold Keck. They were beaten to the overall win only by a GT40; it was another GT40 that split second and fourth, and it was a Porsche, not a Ferrari, that stopped a Ford-powered clean-sweep with its fifth place.

Sebring was unseasonally wet, so wet in fact that the race has gone down in history as the one in which the small, production sports cars almost beat the heavy metal, just on the strength of the appalling conditions. Schlesser was the winner again, this time partnered by Bob Bondurant.

After those first two races, Shelby had 28.8 points in the bag, compared to Ferrari's 4.8. It was turning into as comprehensive a steamroller as Shelby could have wished for after the sour ending of 1964.

Then he went to Monza, in April, and showed what he might have done six months earlier, by taking first and second places with the only two Daytonas entered, with Bondurant partnered by Allen Grant.

At the Spa 500km race immediately after Ferrari's no-show announcement in May, Bondurant's Cobra was beaten into second place in the GT class by Briton Peter Sutcliffe's privately entered Ferrari GTO, while Sir John Whitmore in the other Daytona dropped out of the race. It was one of only two races in which the Daytonas were entered in 1965 and did not win the GT points. The other, unfortunately, was Le Mans, which in some ways counts for as much as all the others put together.

Between Spa and Le Mans, the Daytonas had resumed their winning streak at the Nurburgring 1,000km race, with another

(Right) The Daytonas were out in force at Le Mans in 1965, Grant and Schlesser, who are seen here, failed to finish, as did Miles' and McLaren's GT40.

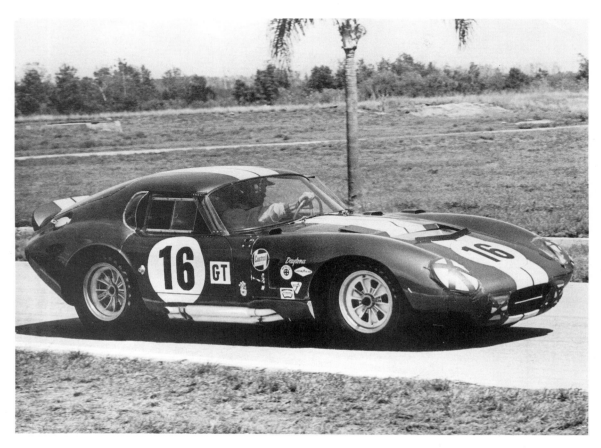

John Timanus and Rick Muther completed a Daytona 1–2–3–4 in the GT class at Sebring in March 1965, setting the Daytonas well on their way for the championship-winning GT season.

fine 1–2–3, led by Bondurant and Schlesser, together again for the first time since winning Sebring. Bondurant also set a new outright GT record for the most demanding circuit in the world, which said a lot for the Daytona's all-round excellence.

Maybe the problem at Le Mans was just that Ford and Shelby's loyalties were finally a bit too compromised. Ford desperately wanted to win overall with the GT40s, now managed by Shelby's old Aston Martin mentor John Wyer, and that was where most of the attention went. The circuit was virtually awash with Ford staff and Ford money, but the Daytonas for once were very much second string. Of the five Daytonas entered, only one finished. That was Dick Thompson and Jack Sear's car, in eighth place overall and second in GT. Anywhere else the result would have looked poor but bearable, but in the glare of Le Mans it was a bit of a disaster, especially as the race was won by an American-entered Ferrari 275LM!

The consolation came just a couple of weeks later – appropriately enough on 4 July, Independence Day – when Shelby finally clinched the FIA World Manufacturers' Championship for GT Cars, with another 1–2 finish, at Reims. Bondurant

Bob Bondurant and Allen Grant led the Daytonas to first and second in the GT class at Monza in 1965, and eighth and ninth places overall, prompting thoughts of what might have happened in the 1964 championship had Monza not been cancelled through Ferrari politics.

and Schlesser did the honours yet again. The Cobra roadsters had done their bit in picking up the points in other events all round Europe where the coupes did not seem to be appropriate entries, but there was no doubt that it was the Daytona's superiority through the past two seasons that had finally done the trick.

They went out as they came in, at the Coppa di Enna in August, with a final 1–2, led by Bondurant again, for the two-car entry, and then they were honourably retired.

Overall, the Daytona's race record was short but impressive. There were only six cars and between them they only raced for two seasons – the last pair were not finished until 1965. They ran to a total of thirty-six entries in fifteen races, seven outings in 1964 and eight in 1965. They won the GT category three times in 1964 and only just missed the championship; they won the category six times in 1965, and the championship with it. At the end of the 1965 season, Shelby retired the Daytonas, to concentrate on helping Ford thrash Ferrari

The best result from the five Daytonas entered at Le Mans in 1965 was eighth place overall, and second in the GT class for Dick Thompson's and Jack Sear's car.

in the outright championship with the GT40.

The age of the brutal and relatively crude sports car, relying on power alone, was drawing to a close, and the age of scientific racing was approaching, with Ford in the forefront. It was the end of the Cobra's international career, but Shelby had achieved what he set out to do.

9 The More Distant Relatives

The last Shelby 427 to be built, CSX3360, was shipped from AC in late December 1966, via Shelby to a New Hampshire Ford dealer, who did not actually sell it until March 1968. That was a couple of months after new Federal emissions and safety laws took effect in the US, which would have killed the Cobra anyway had it not already faded away. It was not quite the last Shelby 427 to be sold 'new', because there were a couple were still in other dealers until at least August 1968.

But then, all of a sudden, the Cobra was gone. The fact was that cars like the Cobra just were not socially acceptable any more, especially not in the USA, and Shelby preferred to let it go rather than to emasculate it to suit the new rules. In any case, he now had his Mustang-based lines to concentrate on, and he was always the type to look forward rather than back.

The Cobra survived a little longer in Europe, with a final, short run of COB6 and COX6 cars along the same lines as the earlier Cobra Britain and Cobra Export numbering system on the leaf-spring chassis. It only ran to thirty-two cars in all, and because the Shelby contract had ended and Ford now owned the Cobra name, they were sold as AC 289s with the combination of small-block engine and coil-spring chassis (though not surprisingly, several were subsequently converted to 427-power).

Strictly speaking, five of that series were not really Cobras either, but at least three of them have since become '427s'. The five were the last five chassis of all, numerically

The AC289 was the last of the real Cobras, built to European requirements in small numbers up to the beginning of 1969.

at least – chassis numbers COX6128 to 6132 – and they were built by AC early in 1968 for Paramount, for use in the film *Monte Carlo or Bust*.

The cars in the film (the sort of film that used to be called 'zany humour') were not Cobras. They were built as ersatz vintage sports cars, caricatured along the lines of a 1930s Mercedes SSK. All the chassis were basically coil-spring 427 Cobra, but all were on extended wheelbases: the first three (which were actually used in the film) on 135in (342.9cm), the last pair (which were bodied with 'vintage' shells but were not used) on 117in (297.2cm).

In the end, they have become a typical example of how something that could not conceivably have been considered a Cobra when it was built could later be transformed into a 'Cobra' purely on the strength of having a chassis number belonging to the original series.

The last of the real AC 289s was completed late in February 1969 and was originally sold in Italy, but even that was not quite the end of the line.

Almost before the real thing went out of production, it was possible to buy replicas, mostly glassfibre-bodied, often pretty crude under the skin, just occasionally quite respectably engineered. Nowadays, there are more replicas of the Cobra on the market than there are of any other car ever made, and they even have their own racing series, but, however good they may be, they are not real Cobras, and both AC and Ford take exceedingly dim views of the use of their trade marks on such cars, especially in advertising them for sale.

Carroll Shelby, as ever, takes a fairly laid-back view. While not knocking replicas as such, he remarked in a *Road & Track* replica road test that he sat in on in August 1983, that he could not understand why the hell anyone would want to build a replica of a car that was already twenty years old when *he* built it.

THE AC MKIV

Since 1982, anyway, you could have bought something rather more than a replica, if something just short of a genuine Shelby or AC Cobra: the AC MkIV.

The MkIV is an all-new car that looks like an original 427, both above and below its exquisitely crafted aluminium bodyshell, which had the full approval of Ford (who are otherwise very sensitive about misuse of the Cobra image), and which legitimately carries the AC badge. Its creator, Brian Angliss, originally described it as being what Shelby might be building if he was still building Cobras today. Shelby himself might take a different view of that, but there's no arguing that the MkIV does have a direct link to the original line.

Angliss, for one thing, is one of the world's best-known Cobra restorers. In the mid-1970s, his business was small and when he set out to restore his first Cobra, he found tremendous problems in finding a great many of the parts he needed, especially body parts. So he started to make the parts he needed for himself, from body panels to chassis components. Once the word got around that he was doing that, and once he had covered his own requirements, Angliss began to supply replacement parts to other Cobra owners and restorers, and he renamed his company Cobra Parts (or CP), with small workshops at Chessington, Surrey.

Eventually, he was making enough parts to build complete cars, possibly as replacements for originals that had been so badly damaged as to be unrepairable, but which could donate some parts – and perhaps even a legitimate chassis number.

Starting in 1974, and having had access to a friend's 427 Cobra to do some proper measuring up, he built his first complete car from parts, and then followed it up with a couple more. He clearly identified them as his own, without any intention to pass them off as originals, although a couple of early purchasers apparently were not quite so scrupulous.

AC Cars had absolutely no reservations about Angliss's integrity, and he had an excellent working relationship with Derek Hurlock, even being appointed sole supplier of genuine replacement AC bodies and panels.

From there, the business (later renamed as Autokraft, with new premises at the old race track at Brooklands), followed a natural growth. By around 1978, while still keeping the highly respected restoration and parts side of the business going, Angliss had seen the scope for building cars in a small series, and he had made contact with a classic car dealer in Chicago who wanted to be involved as backer and sole importer.

Initially, the arrangement looked promising. Angliss delivered the first batch of twelve cars – almost identical to the original 427 – early in 1980. By using original 427 engines it was hoped that they would be accepted as rebuilt cars and not required to face federal type approval problems, but that, unfortunately, was a trifle optimistic and the cars were impounded for some time before eventually being released.

A FEDERALIZED COBRA

Angliss therefore took the plunge and started work to get the car federalized. That would include having to provide 5mph (8kph) bumpers (cleverly done with visually standard bars mounted on shock absorbers within the chassis), providing side intrusion protection, and re-siting the fuel tank closer in behind the cockpit, out of the way of any rear impact. There were lots of small detail requirements, too. The body-supporting chassis superstructure, for instance, was much stronger than the original, the shell was beaten from heavier gauge aluminium, and the cockpit was a bit bigger all round than on the original cars.

The chassis was virtually identical to the original, though (including the faithful Salisbury rear end), and really differed only in the suspension bushing, and the springing and damping settings for the modern tyres, which were mounted on replica Halibrand wheels.

One shrewd move, once Angliss had rejected early thoughts of using Rover V8 power, was to adopt ready-certified running gear. In the first instance, that meant the Ford 352cu in (5,766cc) Windsor V8, and a Ford five-speed manual transmission; later, it more usually meant the 302cu in (4,948cc) Boss Mustang engine, but always with a wide choice of alternatives up to and including the mighty 427.

Using the Ford engines and having to arrange supplies brought Angliss into direct contact with Ford, and they were surprisingly enthusiastic about the car, or at least Edsel Ford II and Michael Kranefuss (of Ford Special Vehicle Operations) were; some other Ford people, and especially the dealers, did not get quite so excited about the possibility of selling the 'Cobra' again as a prestige Ford line to compete with the Corvette.

In spite of that, and the drawn-out process of federalization, of Angliss's admitted inexperience in the American market-place and a split with the original Chicago dealer, Angliss was making real progress. In February 1982, AC Cars Ltd granted him the rights to use the AC logo and to build Cobra-shaped cars for the next twenty-five years – in return for a licensing fee and the right to inspect the quality of the product.

With that, he started production of the next batch of cars, to go on general sale early in 1984. Logically enough he called them the AC MkIV (the MkI having been the 260, the MkII the 289 with rack-and-pinion steering, and the MkIII the coil-spring 427).

Also, in 1984, although the dealers had been surprisingly unenthusiastic about Edsel Ford's 1983 offer of AC MkIV franch-

Dax has a touch more luxury inside than an original Cobra, but the feel is much the same.

Dax's own demonstrator uses a highly tuned Jaguar V12 of almost 6 litres and some 450bhp for 427-like performance.

(Left) There have been good Cobra replicas and bad Cobra replicas. The British-built Dax is one of the best, both for build quality and for visual accuracy. It also has a real Cobra connection in that John Tojeiro, designer of the Ace chassis, is Dax's engineering consultant.

ises, Ford Motor Credit agreed that they would provide customer finance to purchase the cars, which was a big breakthrough for Angliss. He still only had eight US dealers by 1985, though (having rejected several other applicants). Surprisingly, perhaps, not one of them was on the west coast.

Later, in 1987, Ford even granted him permission to use the jealously guarded name Cobra – everywhere, that is, except in the USA, where the product liability implications for Ford as owner of the name were a bit more than they wanted to accept.

While all this had been going on, Angliss had bought a controlling interest in the almost defunct AC Cars Ltd, Ford had bought a controlling interest in AC from Angliss in October 1987, and the MkIV had continued steadily in production towards the 100 car mark. There was every sign too, in mid-1990 after Ford's bombshell announcement that it was about to liquidate AC Cars Ltd, that if anything survived the disputed winding up it would be the MkIV, latterly including an even more limited-edition lightweight version with substantially more power. Echoing an old Shelby 427 theme, Angliss called this version the 8/C.

The car has been universally admired for the quality of its workmanship and for its exceptional finish. It was also widely admired because to all intents and purposes it was very much a Cobra, and given the right engine options, it went like one.

In 1984, *Car and Driver*, with an early 300bhp, 352cu in (5,773cc) engined car, recorded 0–60mph (96.5kph) in 4.4 seconds, 0–100mph (161kph) in 11.2 seconds, a standing quarter in 12.8 seconds and a maximum speed of 140mph (225kph), none of which would have looked far out of place in an early 289 test. They also commented that the handling was much improved, and concluded: 'As a high-performance toy, it's hard to beat. Modern exoticars may be a bit more practical, and several have more refined handling, but few enjoy the AC's

heritage. Still fewer can touch its performance and head-turning ability, and none can match its craftsmanship. For a car nut, the MkIV presses all the right buttons'. That is exactly the sort of thing people always said about the originals.

One final testimonial for the MkIV: Carroll Shelby bought four of the cars a couple of years ago, one for himself, and one each for his three grown-up offspring. That's not too bad a recommendation.

AND THEN THERE WERE THESE

Those, then, including the AC289 and the AC MkIV, are the 'mainstream' Cobras and their derivatives, but there were also a number of cars that, while directly related and often even genuine Cobra below the skin, were somehow or another out of the usual run of things.

A couple of them were legitimately Cobras, but outside the normal numbering system, HEM–6 was a right-hand-drive, leaf-spring Cobra built by AC Cars for European racing in 1964. It was built to full FIA spec, with cutback doors and FIA-style wheelarches and sold, less engine and gearbox, to race entrant 'Tommy' Atkins. It was raced by Roy Salvadori at the 1964 British Grand Prix meeting, to third place in the GT race, and was also driven in British events by Chris during 1964, latterly also being road registered. It has had a very active racing career ever since, nowadays, of course, qualifying as a historic racer!

Another chassis that was completely out of the normal numbering system was A-98, the AC Cars Le Mans coupe, which is described in detail elsewhere, but which was again based on a 289 leaf-spring chassis.

And then there were the Cobra chassis that never had Cobra bodies, but formed the basis for various show cars and prototypes over the years – some just for show, some as

The AC Coupe

One other Cobra coupe that did make it to the starting line was AC's own, on the uniquely numbered chassis A-98.

AC planned it after the reasonable success of their 'fastback' 1963 Le Mans roadster entries, as their entry for Le Mans 1964. In spite of the odd chassis number, it was based on a normal 289 leaf-spring chassis, but in this case with a coupe body styled by AC's Alan Turner. Like Miles's Daytona, it used the body to make the original chassis a good bit stiffer and it was also longer and lower. Its nose was not unlike a GT40's, and its rear quarters not dissimilar to a Ferrari GTO, but its most distinctive feature was small, Mercedes-style 'eyebrows' over each wheelarch, designed to separate the airflows over upper and lower body sections.

It was tested at Le Mans in April and, like the Daytona, showed an alarming tail lightness at very high speeds, which led to a very similar spoiler being added. It also had brake problems, and problems with cockpit cooling.

After one final engine problem back in Britain just before the race, it was given a last shakedown run early in the morning of 14 June 1964 when it proved itself capable of around 185mph (298kph). Unfortunately, the run was on the M1 motorway and, although there was no actual speed limit at the time, the newspapers found out and made rather a big thing of it, and the Ministry of Transport reacted officially with a 'recommendation' that manufacturers did not use Britain's major motorway for testing their cars.

The AC coupe did run at Le Mans in 1964, painted in British racing green and driven by Jack Sears and Peter Bolton. With a 355bhp 289 engine, it was timed at 180mph (289.5kph) on the Mulsanne, compared with an exactly identical speed for one Daytona and around 6mph (9.5kph) quicker for another, but it had a major accident during the sixth hour of the race and was completely wrecked.

AC had planned at one stage to follow up the Le Mans car with a series of maybe a dozen more, but those plans were abandoned. What was left of the crashed car was dismantled and stored at AC for several years before being acquired by British Cobra enthusiast Barrie Bird in the early 1970s and eventually finished to absolutely correct 1964 Le Mans spec during 1984.

possible Cobra replacements.

Two of them were commissioned by Shelby in 1966, from styling house Ghia of Turin, later acquired by Ford via De Tomaso, as part of the process of turning the Mangusta into the production Pantera. The Shelby chassis were numbered CSX5001 and CSX5002, which again broke slightly with the production numbering system of 2-prefixes for leaf-springs, 3-prefixes for coil-springs, and 6-prefixes for export cars. In spite of their significance as one-off Ghia cars, both seem to have gone the way of everything else with a CSX chassis number, as '427s'.

Originally, one was built purely as a roadster, the other had a removable hard top, and both had very stylish interiors with a lot more comfort options than any Cobra;

it even had wind-up windows!

The Ghia Cobras were unveiled at the Turin Show in November 1965. With a tall windscreen and faired-in rectangular headlights, they were much more angular and sharp-edged, much more typically 1960s, much more typically Italian than the aggressively bulbous Cobra, but they were not such bad looking cars for all that. They were also not unlike the Frua-bodied AC 428 that AC built on the lengthened 427 chassis for a few years after Cobra production ended.

The only real Cobra link for the AC 428 is the modified 427 coil-spring chassis and Cobra running gear, and the fact that AC built it as a direct follow-on. In fact it overlapped Cobra production by a couple of years, shown as a convertible prototype at

The AC MkIV is slightly less than a real Shelby Cobra, but very much more than a replica. Brian Angliss's interpretation of how the Cobra would be in 1990 is built on original tooling and body bucks and is as close to an original as possible.

The interior of the MkIV has that familiar minimalism.

You can have a choice of Fords under the bonnet of your MkIV, from the popular 302cu in Boss Mustang engine as shown here, right up to a genuine 427 side-oiler – at a price.

A brand-new Cobra.

Beyond the MkIV, Brian Angliss started a very limited run of lightweight models, even more in line with the original Cobra ethic.

In 1965, Ghia produced two styling exercises on the Cobra, as pure roadster and with removable hardtop. The lines are classically mid-60s Italian, the interior as seen in the hardtop car is very luxurious, but the Ghia Cobras never went beyond being show cars.

the London Motor Show in March 1965, as a fastback coupe at the Geneva Show in March 1966 and launched into production for early 1967. It was a good-looking car, more luxuriously equipped than the Cobra and with more space. That was possible because the main change AC made was to lengthen the chassis by some 6in, and soften the suspension in keeping with the Grand Tourer role. It was not a bad car at all, but AC only built around fifty-eight coupes and twenty-eight convertibles before the 428 went out of production altogether in 1973. It was finally, and inevitably, the victim of the world oil crisis – 7-litre engines do not go with frugality.

The 428 idea, incidentally, had probably been floating around AC for some time before that car appeared, because AC also built another more civilized roadster as early as 1963, loosely based on a leaf-spring chassis. That was chassis number MA-200, the MA presumably standing for Marcewski, after AC's Polish-born designer, Z. T. Marcewski – the man who John Tojeiro had taken out and frightened in the prototype Ace!

AC were probably looking for a European cousin for the Cobra, with a few more creature comforts, slightly less rabid performance and gentler road manners for their more traditional customers. Marcewski devised a car with strut-type rear suspension with wide-angle wishbones, a steering rack moved above and behind the front suspension and a very strange choice of engines. As designed, it should have had a 2-litre flat-six AC engine, designed by Alan Turner in the early 1960s and of which a few examples had actually been built. They were not very promising, with rough running and a tendency to break, so MA-200 inevitably ended up with a Ford 289 V8. Clothed in an Italianate roadster body (which later led to some people thinking, wrongly, that it was a 428 prototype), and registered 6000 PE, it was used on the road for some time by AC

sales manager Jock Henderson. It had overheating problems, problems with the complex chassis and rear suspension, and Ford would not, in any case, have been keen to supply engines for a car to compete with the Cobra, so that was as far as it went, although the one-off prototype still exists.

THE ELECTRIC ALTERNATIVE

Strangest of all of them, perhaps, was the EFX series of cars. They were a project that did not even start until long after the original was out of production, in 1969, when Electric Fuel Propulsion Inc of Ferndale, Michigan, were looking for a basis for an experimental, electric-powered car. They never had Cobra bodies, and they could not conceivably be called Cobras in any true sense of the name, but they did have connections.

In 1969, Electric Fuel Propulsion had approached an independent engineering consultant by the name of Bob Negstadt, and if the name sounds familiar it is because he was the same Bob Negstadt who helped Klaus Arning and Ford's computers to design the suspension for the coil-spring 427 Cobra, back in 1963.

Negstadt, probably quite rightly given the scale of the project, suggested to Electric Fuel Propulsion that instead of spending vast amounts of money on starting from scratch, they could do worse than to adapt a 427-type chassis to their needs.

Accordingly, AC, with the tooling still available, of course, built eight special chassis for the company, virtually identical to the out-of-production original except for a modified layout between the two, big, frame tubes, to accommodate a large collection of batteries. There were no normal engine mounts, and a rather lower final-drive ratio to cope with something less than the old 427's 475bhp.

AC's own final variation on the Cobra theme was the 428, styled by Frua over a coil-spring chassis and '427' running gear. The 428 was a pretty car but badly timed with the oil crises of the early 1970s.

AC went for luxury and modern gimmicks with the 428, but to little avail.

The Cobra lives on . . .

Whatever the problems with the electric 'Cobras', no more chassis were built, and the ones that were, numbered EFX501 to EFX508, have mostly been used up since, either for conversion to 'new' 427s or as parts sources for badly damaged 427s. They serve best of all to show what extraordinary lengths people will go to to possess something even tenuously related to a real Cobra.

That is the sort of car it was and is.

10 Driving and Ownership

For the drivers and owners of the AC Cobra, there is some good news and some bad news.

The good news is that the Cobra, 289 or 427, is every bit as beautiful in the flesh and every bit as exciting to drive as anything ever written about it would have you believe. It is also a relatively simple car, robust in almost every respect (except its damage-prone aluminium skin), with a production-based engine and with virtually all parts available – at a price.

The bad news is that unless you already own a Cobra, putting one into your garage is now extremely expensive and, as time goes by, even finding Cobras for sale is becoming rarer.

Look back at the numbers. Between February 1962 and August 1968, a total of almost exactly 1000 Cobras was built. Just 655 leaf-spring cars were built in total. Seventy-five with the 260 engine, 580 with the 289, and the majority of 260s were retrofitted with the 289 as soon as it was available so that original 260-engined Cobras are now all but non-existent.

Of those totals, only sixty-two of the 260s were sold supposedly as pure road cars, and only 515 289s, of which sixty were COB/COX European-spec road cars. The rest are listed by the Shelby American World Registry as starting life as race cars of one kind or another, and any surviving car with a reasonable race history will be even more expensive than a typical road car.

Of the total 348 coil-spring cars, just 260 were road cars (plus most of the 32 COB/COX cars) and the rest were competition cars, including the thirty-one that were officially designed as semi-competition roadsters. The Cobra is a rare beast.

In the late 1960s, when it was just a recently out of production sports car, prices were rock-bottom, say less than £1,500 for a good 289. From there, they have moved inexorably upwards at a rate which latterly accelerated almost as quickly as the cars themselves. In the early 1970s, you could still buy a Cobra for £2–3,000, but by the mid-1970s you would already have been looking in the £7,000 region for a good car; by the early 1980s a 289 with provenance was up to £12–13,000 and the rarer 427 had already passed £20,000. By the mid 1980s, £30,000 was a more realistic starting price.

Into the 1990s, prices are even more dependent on history as Cobras come onto the market even less frequently. The vast majority, of course, were sold initially in the USA and that is where they still are. It is likely that there were never more than around eighty Cobras in total in Britain at any one time, and now there are even less than that, with a mere handful of 427s. Values, however, are such that you are no more likely to find a 'bargain' Cobra in the USA than in Britain or Europe, and such sales as there are are likely to have potential buyers worldwide.

That is reflected in typical mid-1990 prices of as much as £150,000 for a good 289 even without any special individual history, or close to double that for a genuinely 427-engined 427. Those prices, too, at the time of writing, are still upwardly mobile.

Cobras were road cars, but were racers underneath; here the author drives John Atkins' racing 289.

HOW GENUINE IS GENUINE?

Most of the cars that survive (and that, in fact, is most of the cars built) are restored to top-end-of-the-market condition, or are very good originals. Many Cobras, understandably enough, have had accidents of greater or lesser severity in their time, but as the Cobra became rarer and more valuable, very few were actually scrapped. Now, virtually everything that ever had any kind of Cobra chassis number (including tenuous claimants like the electric-car chassis and the long-wheelbase Paramount film chassis) has already been rebuilt into a 'Cobra', and the rising market means that basket-case Cobras or farmyard 'discoveries' are things of the past.

The Shelby American Automobile Club has an excellent set of definitions to cover virtually every category of car. 'Original' describes a car whose main frame tubes and pieces carrying the serial numbers have not been replaced or altered. (There are numerous pieces which should carry identification numbers, including the chassis itself, the bonnet and boot catches, the door hinges, the transmission tunnel, and the rear bulkhead. The numbers identify both chassis and major body parts as being original.)

The next category is 'original/restored', referring to a car having less than half its original substructure or bodywork replaced, but *not* the main frame tubes or other pieces carrying serial numbers.

'Original/rebodied' defines a car having more than half its original substructure or bodywork replaced, but again, *not* the main frame tubes or any other pieces carrying numbers.

'Replica', to SAAC, means a car that has been rebuilt substantially to original specifications (including replacement of the main frame tubes) but in which some part of the original car existed prior to the rebuild, and documentable paperwork such as a traceable bill-of-sale, a registration or such, still exists.

All those, to a greater or lesser extent, are legitimate Cobras, and some heavily damaged competition cars in particular will fall into the latter definitions while still having perfectly legitimate histories, but outside of all those definitions are a number of categories which can best be called forgery.

The Cobra, by virtue of its relatively simple mechanical make-up, its production-based engine and transmission, and nowadays its very high value, is a car which is increasingly often faked.

Some fakes are imitation without intent at deception. There are a vast number of kit-car Cobra lookalikes which make no attempt to duplicate the real thing under their (usually glassfibre) skins, and such cars are almost invariably such bits-and-pieces creations that there is no real likelihood at all of their being passed off as the real thing. There is also, of course, the AC MkIV, which is very much a Cobra from the ground up, but which has never made any attempt to pass itself off as 'original'.

And then there are the much less scrupulous copies, the outright frauds in many cases. These can be cars created with an absolute minimum of genuine but non-numbered parts, but claiming a genuine provenance. Such provenance is often based on a real chassis number whose record is either non-existent or so vague as to be open to a fraudulent claim of ownership. They can even be cars created from absolute zero, without so much as a nut and bolt in them that has ever been on a genuine Cobra, but in the way just described even these cars can have fraudulently 'adopted' a real identity. The SAAC colourfully describe the last category as 'air cars'.

The fact is that it should be very difficult to be caught with a non-genuine Cobra. Both AC's chassis records and SAAC's registers are far more detailed than the information that exists for many classic cars, and SAAC

in particular are willing to give potential buyers all available advice.

That said, there are already, without doubt, a number of fraudulent 'Cobras' in existence, and in future there are likely to be more, simply because there are still some less than honest people in the world. The rule must be 'buyer beware'.

CARING FOR THE COBRA

Once you have your Cobra, it is a relatively undemanding supercar to look after. Where virtually every mechanical item on the likes of a Ferrari or a Lamborghini or the more technically exotic classics can be a nightmare to maintain and replace, the majority of the Cobra's major driveline components are nothing more daunting than Ford or Jaguar/Salisbury sourced.

Equally fortuitously, what remains was virtually all simple fabrication (the tubular chassis, the aluminium body, et al.), and what was fabricated in the first instance can generally be fabricated again by skilled craftsmen.

That is not to say that Cobra restoration and maintenance are cheap; they are very far from it, because the market is limited, highly specialized, and does depend on high levels of skill and craftsmanship, but the Cobra is now a car that can be kept on road or track with few major problems, which makes it a car that can be used as intended.

It is also, basically, a very reliable car. It had its early breakage problems, as we have seen, but the fact is that Shelby engineered most of those out as the build programme went along, for the very simple reason that racing cars that break do not win. Many of the lessons learned, too, were retrospectively noted and adjustments made accordingly by owners of early cars.

Corrosion problems with the Cobra are fairly limited. There is always the possibility of rust in the main frame tubes, but it is not a common problem and the tubes are very strong. More of a problem is the possibility of rust in the outriggers to the main frame tubes, or corrosion caused by chemical reaction where the aluminium of the body shell meets the steel of the frame. All such problems are curable with an appropriate injection of money and craftsmanship.

Mechanically, none of the Cobras has major problems. Even in fairly advanced states of tune, the engines are very reliable given proper maintenance and a degree of mechanical sympathy. That should not be difficult, as the performance of any Cobra is such that it will only rarely be driven to its full potential. The Cobra philosophy, remember, is based more on lazy, lightly-stressed power from a big engine in a lightweight chassis, than on extreme and unreliable tuning.

The Cobra gearboxes are equally reliable, in spite of the amount of power and torque they have to transmit. Lower gear syncromesh does tend to get tired after a while, but it is very unusual for any Cobra gearbox actually to break in normal use. Ditto the final drive, which in essence survived unchanged from 260 to 427.

In a nutshell, a well-maintained Cobra, driven with the understanding that heavy-handedness will put very substantial mechanical stresses on the car, should present very few running problems.

ON THE ROAD

That just leaves a car to be enjoyed for its attractive simplicity and staggering performance, and make no mistake, Cobra performance is still staggering even by the most extreme 1990s supercar standards.

It *is* a simple car: the cockpit has two seats with no possibility whatsoever of squeezing anyone else in. The 427 is a few inches bigger all round than the 289, inside as well as out, but even the 289 has enough cockpit space to allow a comfortably straight armed driving position. The pedals are quite small (and have the AC logo cast in, even on the 427) but there is not a great deal of space around your feet, and in the 427 in particular, the pedals are pushed a long way off-centre by the big transmission tunnel.

There is little or no trim. For starters, there are no external door handles, just a catch or a leather-cord pull inside the door — which itself is no more than a thin aluminium shell on a minimal tubular frame, with an elasticated map-pocket if the car is not a totally stripped-out racer. There is carpet on the floor and the seats are leather, but you could not call it luxurious.

The seat backs are very low by modern standards, which means there is little or no shoulder support; but simple and flat-looking as they are, they are quite comfortable for the sort of shortish journey a Cobra is most likely to be used for. If you are planning a long run, too, be warned that luggage space in the boot is strictly limited and, in the glovebox, is even more limited.

Nor is the Cobra a very appealing wet-weather car: notwithstanding the delicacy required to tame the performance on rain-slick surfaces, the hood is a laughably old-fashioned frame-and-cover affair that is a trial to put up quickly and usually hopelessly flapping or leaking even when it is in place.

The rest leaves you in little doubt that the Cobra is more racer than road car, even when the actual example is supposedly more road car than racer.

Instrumentation and switches are comprehensive but scattergun in their layout. The 289 and 427 dashboards were pretty well identical, with the usual proviso that many

(Overleaf) The Cobra's performance was stunning, thanks to the combination of minimal weight and ample Ford V8 power.

cars, particularly those with a racing history, have 'bespoke' instrument and switch layouts. In general, there is everything there that you could possibly wish to read: the larger dials behind the steering wheel are speedo and tachometer, and in the centre are smaller gauges for battery charge, fuel level, water and oil temperatures, oil pressure, and usually a clock. All the instruments are classic white on black and easy to read, but the switches are a bit less clear, with a well-spread mix of push/pull and toggle switches, mainly without any labelling.

The handbrake lever sprouts alongside the transmission tunnel. On the 289 the gearlever is short and well forward; on the 427 it is usually a long lever sprouting forwards from a base set right back in the transmission tunnel, that is in fact, the standard Ford lever turned back-to-front from the position it would be in if the transmission was in a rather bigger saloon car, where it originated.

The controls are not particularly heavy, assuming you are applying hairy-chested 1960s sports car criteria rather than modern, power-with-everything saloon car standards. From the moment you start the engine, though, there is no doubt at all that the performance will be very heavyweight.

There is none of the thoroughbred temperament of a Ferrari V12 or its ilk about the Ford V8s, either big-block or small-block, none of that sewing-machine lightness overlaid with the mechanical clamour of multiple cams and valves and thousands of tiny parts working in delicate unison. No, the Cobra V8s are big, simple engines, glorious but unsophisticated muscle that rocks the whole car as you blip the throttle.

Even before you select a gear and drop the clutch, there is no possible doubt that the Cobra's performance will be monstrous. And indeed it is, but it is also dual-natured. With its immense flexibility and two-stage carburettor opening, even a 427 can be deceptively docile. It will rumble around with no

major drama at low speeds, in any gear you choose, heavier through the wheel but not impossibly so, and quite manageable even in traffic.

Ask it to go, however, and the acceleration is quite simply staggering. Such figures as we have quoted elsewhere, with 0–60mph (96.5kph) acceleration close to four seconds, 0–100mph (161kph) in barely a blink over ten seconds, are formidable, and feel it. Maybe the 289 feels lighter and more responsive in its pick-up than the 427, and the 427 more phenomenally flexible in its mid-to-top-range thunder, but frankly all of it is well outside normal realms of experience. Almost the most impressive thing of all is not the standing start acceleration but a colossal mid-range flexibility that makes the gearbox all but superfluous.

The ride is harsh but bearable on the short-travel springing of the leaf-spring cars, better by far on the more progressive, longer-travel coil-spring models, good by racing car standards, passable by heavy-metal sports car standards.

The handling is surprisingly forgiving, given all the awesome power and the relative paucity of outright grip on period tyres. The weight distribution is very slightly rearward biased, but so slightly that you would be hard pressed to notice.

Set up for the road, the Cobra has plenty of cautionary initial understeer – understandably so with a big V8 up front that would be quite content to keep going in a straight line. Hardly surprisingly, there is also the ultimate option of power oversteer in most circumstances, and a skilled driver would steer the Cobra equally effectively with throttle or highly communicative, pleasantly quick steering, or a practised combination of both.

The brakes, too, are powerful and solid, because they are big and the car is light; they take a hefty push, but they work. So all in all, the Cobra is not a difficult car to drive adequately well, but it is a challenging and intimidating car to wring the last ounce of performance from.

That, above all, is what makes the Cobra great: its ability to flatter an average driver and reward a brilliant one. Its utter simplicity and singleness of purpose are its long suits. No amount of sophistication in later supercars challenges the ultimate thrill of the Cobra's formidable power, the immediacy of everything in its repertoire. When the rules changed and made cars like the Cobra obsolete so far as future production was concerned, the motoring world lost something unique.

11 Dodge Viper and Shelby After the Cobra

By the time the Cobra went out of production in 1966, Carroll Shelby, never a man to rest long on his laurels, was already applying his considerable talents in several other directions.

In 1963 and 1964 he had had a brief flirtation with Can-Am racing by putting Cobra engines into Cooper chassis in a short and not very successful run of mid-engined sports racing cars which were dubbed King Cobras. He had been a partner in the early 1960s in Dan Gurney's All-American Racers team, which had a degree of success in Grand Prix racing, and he had become deeply involved in Ford's GT40 programme, perhaps the ultimate expression of Total Performance.

Ford's GT project was as much a result of Enzo Ferrari's obduracy as Shelby's Cobras had been. By the time the first Cobras were appearing, in 1962, Iacocca, the force behind Ford's racing effort, had set his sights on winning events as diverse as Indianapolis and Le Mans. Relatively speaking, Indy was home ground for Ford and winning really meant providing a winning engine to an established team. Le Mans was something else, a start-from-scratch operation against the background of an old racing adage that said however good you are, it takes three years to win at Le Mans.

Iacocca did not want to wait three years, so Ford tried the ultimate short-cut, to buy out Ferrari, creating Ford-Ferrari road cars and Ferrari-Ford race cars. It came very close to happening, and in the late stages

Don Frey, Shelby's ally from Ford in creating the Cobra, was heavily involved in the negotiations, but in the end it all foundered on the familiar rocks of Ferrari's stubborn autonomy: he still wanted to run the racing show.

Up to a point, Ford were willing to accede, but then Ferrari demanded that Ford could race *only* via Ferrari-Ford. Whether or not it was a direct attack on Shelby, it would have meant that Ford could not run the Cobra, and that was already a powerful part of their image building, so the deal was off. Ferrari tried to re-open the negotiations a few weeks later, but Ford had already decided to go the Shelby route and whip Ferrari on their own terms.

They started looking for a basis for their new world beater, and Shelby was delegated to point them in the right direction. When he went to Le Mans in 1963, the two Cobras in the race were AC and Hugus entries, while Shelby was left largely free to go fact-finding for Ford.

In the end, Ford based their first GT40 on an English Lola. Shelby took the leading role in co-ordinating the European and US sides of the operation (with the European programme run by his old Aston Martin mentor John Wyer), and was also to be the distributor of the customer cars.

The GT programme started slowly and none too promisingly in 1964, but the blow was softened for Ford by the successes of the Cobras. For 1965, the GT40s appeared in Shelby colours, revised and developed by

Even while the Cobra was still racing, Shelby was becoming heavily involved with Ford's GT40 programme, co-ordinating Ford's multi-million dollar US and European operations and providing the engineering input to turn theory into race-winning practice. Shelby was back at Le Mans with these GT40s for the 50th birthday of the race.

much the same team as had developed the Cobra and the Daytona, and they immediately started winning. It *did* take Ford three years to win Le Mans, but from the start of 1965 the GT programme was a steamroller success, with Shelby and Wyer leading the way.

Wyer was also there for the later Ford-powered Gulf-Mirage Le Mans victories, but Shelby's direct involvement with the GTs stopped in 1967, after the second Le Mans win when Ford, having proved their point, withdrew from sports car racing.

Shelby had a production link with Ford too, in the Shelby Mustangs, even while he

was still building Cobras and running GT40s. The recently launched bread-and-butter Mustang was doing well, but it was not tempting the seriously sporty young American away from the Corvette, because it was not a proper performance car, so Ford called in Shelby again. In fact it was Ray Geddes, another prominent figure in the birth of the Cobra, who suggested Shelby should see Iacocca about doing something to improve the Mustang's image, and the ever enthusiastic Iacocca who gave the go-ahead.

As was normal around Total-Performance-dominated Ford in those mid-60s days, racing was the bottom line. Shelby managed to

The GT40 as it first appeared in early 1964 was based on a British Lola design, considerably refined by Ford. In the early days it had endless problems and simply could not match the Ferraris, but by 1965 Shelby had turned it into a winner, simultaneously starting the decline of the Daytona in racing.

get a performance Mustang accepted by the SCCA as a sports car rather than a saloon, so long as he could make a two-seater version and so long as Ford would build at least 100 of them. Thus was the Shelby GT-350 born.

Shelby did not dream the name as he had with the Cobra, but it had nothing to do with either capacity or performance. Struggling to think of something to call the car, Shelby asked chief engineer Phil Remington how far he reckoned it was to a nearby building. Remington suggested about 350 feet, and that is how the car got its name. It also had the Cobra name and logo on the engine and the steering wheel boss.

Ken Miles did much of the development

work, Brock did the cosmetics, and also involved was Ford's Klaus Arning (the man who was soon to help develop the coil-spring chassis for the 427 Cobra). The GT-350 was homologated in January 1965 and went on sale within weeks. In much the same way as AC with the Cobra, Ford supplied the basic car and Shelby provided the specialist touches to complete it, adding power (courtesy of the Cobra parts bin) and throwing away superfluous weight, in his spacious new premises at Los Angeles Airport.

Shelby was a big operation by this time and the Mustangs would make him far more money than the Cobra ever did. They sold in much bigger numbers, of course, including the competition cars which promptly went

Shelby Mustang GT-350 was Shelby's way of putting some pep into the Mustang line for Ford. This Mustang and the ones that followed it made a good deal of money for Shelby but also in the end led to his split with Ford.

out and dominated their class in SCCA racing. Shelby briefly offered a Paxton supercharged option, but the most remarkable variant was the GT-350H, a car built specifically for Hertz, and inevitably nicknamed the Rent-a-Racer. Having expected to sell Hertz a few dozen, Shelby eventually received an order for 1,000, to sit alongside Hertz's Corvettes for Hertz Sports Car Club members to rent. Ford liked that.

In 1966, Shelby prepared a four-seat Mustang for the SCCA's new Trans-Am saloon series, and started winning heavily there, too. In 1967, he added the 428-engined GT-500 to the range. That was not so much a faster car as a more refined one, pushing production up even further, but the Shelby Mustangs were already starting to suffer Ford's shift of emphasis away from real performance and towards cosmetic image.

For 1968 (by which time Shelby was also

setting up a three-car Toyota 2000GT racing programme and thinking of a successor for the Cobra), Mustang production was moved away from Shelby and eventually in-house to Ford. By the time the series ended in late 1969, well over 14,000 Shelby Mustangs had been built, which did no harm at all to Shelby's bank balance.

They did, finally, do a lot of harm to Shelby's special relationship with Ford. As the Mustang operation grew, Ford took an increasingly proprietorial role, including sending their own production people and dictating the specifications of the cars. On the other hand, they were looking increas-

ingly to Ghia and De Tomaso rather than to Shelby for a showroom successor to the Cobra which, as described elsewhere, eventually led to the Mangusta and the Pantera.

Shelby was also now having difficulty in being recognized by the authorities (especially in California, ironically) as a separate entity from Ford, and that made him feel uneasy. Shelby American was split into three elements: Shelby Automotive and Shelby Parts and Accessories taking the manufacture and supply sides to Michigan, and Shelby Racing staying in California, but with ever less work to do for Ford. Late in 1969, Ford announced a 75 per cent cut in

The Sunbeam Tiger combined small-block Ford power with a mass-produced chassis from the UK Chrysler off-shoot, Sunbeam. In a way, it was even more of what Shelby had intended his roadgoing Cobra to be than the real Cobra was, and Shelby still regards it with some affection.

their racing budgets, which effectively meant the end of any racing link with Shelby. Shelby himself negotiated his way out of the Mustang operation, officially because legislation was making such cars harder to build, in reality because both the car and the bureaucracy were turning into something he did not want to work with.

While he had still had the remnants of Ford backing, Shelby had tried another mid-engined Can-Am racer, the Cougar-Cobra, developed in Britain by Len Terry, but the unconventional car was a resounding failure. He had also dabbled with a road/race Cobra successor in the Lone Star, also built in Britain, this time by Len Bailey. The car, with lift-off hard-top, was 289-powered, with the engine mounted midships in a monocoque chassis with all-independent coil and wishbone suspension, but it was bulbous and evil-handling and was abandoned after the first prototype stage.

With considerably more success, Shelby had also found time in the thick of the Cobra and GT40 days to create the Sunbeam Tiger – a Ford V8-engined version of the Sunbeam Alpine, which Shelby himself has always had a great affection for.

Having been approached by US-based Sunbeam executive Ian Garrad, Shelby developed the Tiger in a matter of weeks and on a shoestring budget for the Rootes Group. Rootes was just being turned into the British outpost of Chrysler, but Shelby gave the car the faithful Ford 'small-block' V8, just as in the Cobra, and the car was launched at the New York Show in April 1964.

The Tiger was never quite so extreme as the Cobra, but it was a good deal more refined, a lot cheaper, and a fine, quick car in its own right. It started with the 260 engine in 164bhp trim and got a 200bhp 289 for 1967, but that was the last year of production. Shelby did not actually build the car, that was done by Jensen in England. In the end, it was the victim of corporate politics after just over 7,000 had been built

because, as Chrysler gained more influence over Sunbeam, they simply found it harder to market a car with 'Powered by Ford' badges on its flanks.

Having severed his Ford links, Shelby went into the 1970s with only tenuous connections with the motoring world. Carroll Shelby Enterprises marketed magnesium wheels for both cars and motor cycles, Shelby maintained his Goodyear tyre connections and had a Lincoln/Mercury dealership, but his other interests were as diverse as owning real estate, marketing a fearsomely hot chilli mix, hunting in Africa, and farming thoroughbred horses and exotic birds (not chickens) on a huge ranch in east Texas. He also bought a share in another Texan cattle ranch, some 200,000 acres around the abandoned mining town of Terlingua, and sharing part of its boundaries with Big Bend national park. Shelby turned the ghost town into a sort of outward bound school, teaching everything from farming to auto and aero engineering to underprivileged boys, and thus created the Terlingua Boys Ranch – advertised on his later racing cars through the Terlingua Racing Team.

In spite of undergoing a number of heart operations, Shelby just could not give up working and, inevitably, that eventually brought him back into mainstream motoring. The catalyst was Iacocca and the company was Chrysler, the people he had indirectly done the Sunbeam Tiger for.

Iacocca, frustrated by Ford's tamer image of the 1970s, left them late in 1978 and walked straight into the hot seat at Chrysler – a company with massive problems at the time and seemingly little future. Within a few years, Iacocca had turned Chrysler around – and in 1982 he brought Carroll Shelby on to the scene with his own 'R&D' operation to inject some sporting life into Chrysler's generally rather dull range.

From a necessarily low-key, low-budget start, Shelby moved quickly from not much more than cosmetic upgrades to some extremely sporty small and front-drive cars for the Dodge division. Shelby has deliberately worked on cars for the man in the street rather than the old-style, thinly disguised racers and, nowadays, the Shelby nameplate is on all manner of Dodges from the Dodge Shadow-based CSX front-wheel-drive baby to the Shelby Dakota pick-up.

His name was also prominent at the Detroit Show in January 1989, when Chrysler showed off a spectacular sports car that they had badged as the Dodge Viper. It was a brutal-looking open two-seater with side exhausts and a V10 engine. The name Viper was confirmation that Chrysler thought of the car as their 'Cobra for the 1990s', and Shelby of course, was on the list of instigators.

With prospective buyers virtually queuing up to offer deposits, Chrysler had little option but to think of developing the show car for production. Like Ford with the Cobra, they needed the image boost, but on a minimum budget. With an engine already available and by keeping the rest of the car as simple as possible, Chrysler reckoned to keep development costs down to mere millions of dollars rather than the hundreds of millions that a typical full-scale launch involves.

In the 1990s, even that involves rather more than the tiny handful of people who created the Cobra, but Chrysler president Bob Lutz reckons the job was done by a team of no more than fifty people, working with as much co-operation and as little bureaucracy as possible in a single facility where the prototypes were actually built. They had an overall budget, but within that had almost complete autonomy in deciding where to spend it.

The concept seemed to work; because in May 1990, at the end of an 'image-boosting' tour, Chrysler chairman Iacocca announced that the car *would* go into production and be on sale by the beginning of 1992, tamed a little from the show car perhaps, but still with the Cobra spirit, and with Shelby keeping a watching brief, of course . . .

SHELBY COBRA 427 SPECIFICATION

PRODUCTION 1965–1968

Body type	Two-seater roadster; all-aluminium
Chassis	Large-diameter twin-tube ladder frame with tubular suspension mountings and tubular superstructure
Engine type	Ford V8
Capacity	'427' is actually 426cu in (6,984cc) '428' is actually 427 cu in (6,991cc) (both engine types used in Cobra 427)
Bore	'427', 4.24in (107.7mm); '428', 4.13in (104.9mm)
Stroke	'427', 3.78in (96.0mm); '428', 3.98in (101.1mm)
Compression ratio	'427', 10.4:1; '428', 10.5:1
Cylinders	Cast-iron block, five main bearings, single central camshaft
Cylinder heads	Cast-iron, two valves per cylinder, operated by pushrods
Fuel system	Single four-barrel Holley carburettor (four twin-choke downdraught Weber carburettors optional)
Maximum power	'427' 425bhp @ 6,500rpm; '428' 390bhp @ 5,200rpm
Maximum torque	'427' 480lb ft @ 3,500rpm; '428' 475lb ft @ 3,700rpm
Bhp per litre	'427' 60.8 (1.0bhp per cu in); '428' 55.8 (0.91bhp per cubic inch)
Gearbox type	Ford 'top-loader' four-speed manual, all synchromesh
Gear ratios	Fourth: 1:00 Second: 1.69 Third: 1:29 First: 2:32 Reverse: 2:32
Final drive ratio	3:31 (numerous options available)
Clutch	Single dry-plate, hydraulic operation
Front suspension	Independent, by unequal-length upper and lower wishbones, with coil springs and telescopic dampers
Rear suspension	Independent, by unequal-length upper and lower wishbones, with additional lower trailing links, coil springs and telescopic dampers
Brakes	Solid discs front and rear
Steering	Rack and pinion
Wheels & tyres	7.5J × 15in centre-lock, pin-drive, cast-magnesium Halibrand wheels (later up to 9.5J × 15 at rear); 8.5 × 15in tyres (later up to 11.4 × 15in at rear)
Overall length	156.0in (3,962mm)
Overall width	68.0in (1,727mm)
Overall height	49.0in (1,244mm)
Wheelbase	90.0in (2,286mm)
Track	Front: 56.0in (1,422mm) Rear: 56.0in (1,422mm)
Ground clearance	4.5in (114mm)
Fuel tank capacity	15.0 gallons (18.0 US gallons) (68 litres)
Unladen weight	2,350lb (1,066kg)
Power-to-weight ratio	405.1bhp per ton

Performance (typical figures for 427-engined car)

Maximum speed	165mph (265kph)
0–60mph (0–96.5kph)	4.2 seconds
0–100mph (0–161kph)	10.3 seconds
Standing ¼-mile	12.4 seconds
Fuel consumption	10.0mpg

SHELBY AC COBRA 289 SPECIFICATION

PRODUCTION 1962–1965

Body type	Two-seater roadster; all-aluminium
Chassis	Twin-tube ladder frame with box-section suspension mountings and tubular superstructure
Engine type	Ford V8
Capacity	289cu in (4,736cc) [260cu in (4,261cc) up to chassis no CSX2074]
Bore	4.0in (101.6mm); 3.80in (96.5mm)
Stroke	2.87in (72.9mm)
Compression ratio	11.6:1
Cylinders	Thinwall cast-iron block, five main bearings, single central camshaft
Cylinder heads	Cast-iron, two valves per cylinder, operated by pushrods
Fuel system	Single four-barrel Holley carburettor (four twin-choke downdraught Weber carburettors optional)
Maximum power	271bhp @ 6,000rpm (260bhp @ 5,800rpm from 260cu in)
Maximum torque	314lb ft @ 3,400rpm (269lb ft @ 4,800rpm from 260cu in)
Bhp per litre	57.2 (0.94bhp per cubic inch) [61.0 (1.0bhp per cubic inch for 260cu in 4,261cc)]
Gearbox type	Borg-Warner four-speed manual, all synchromesh
Gear ratios	Fourth: 1:00 Second: 1.78 Third: 1:41 First: 2:36 Reverse: 2:36
Final drive ratio	3:77 (numerous options available)
Clutch	Single dry-plate, hydraulic operation
Front suspension	Independent, by lower wishbones and transverse leafspring upper link, telescopic dampers
Rear suspension	Independent by lower wishbones and transverse leafspring upper link, telescopic dampers
Brakes	Solid discs front and rear
Steering	Rack and pinion (worm and sector up to chassis no CSX2125)
Wheels & tyres	6J × 15in (15.2 × 381mm) centre-lock wire wheels; 7.35 × 15 crossply or 185 × 15in radial tyres
Overall length	151.5in (3,848mm)
Overall width	61.0in (1,549mm)
Overall height	49.0in (1,244mm)
Wheelbase	90.0in (2,286mm)
Track	Front: 51.5in (1,308mm) Rear: 52.5in (1,333mm)
Ground clearance	5.0in (127mm)
Fuel tank capacity	15.0 gallons (18.0 US gallons) (68 litres)
Unladen weight	2,170lb (984kg)
Power-to-weight ratio	279.7bhp per ton

Performance (typical figures for 289)

Maximum speed	138mph (222kph)
0–60mph (0–96.5kph)	5.5 seconds
0–100mph (0–161kph)	13.0 seconds
Standing ¼-mile	13.9 seconds
Fuel consumption	15.1mpg

Index

AAA 71
AC, cars
  2-litre saloon *35*, 36, 58
  10hp 26–7, *28*
  16/80 *34*
  289 *9*, 10, 11, 12, 79, 126,
    131, *136*, 173, *173*, 174–8
  428 7, 40, *41*, 134, 179, *184*,
    185
  Ace 6, 7, 11, 14, 30, 33, 37,
    39, 40, 41, 45, 46–65, *50*,
    54, *56*, *57*, *59*, *64*, 69, 70, 74,
    75, 80, 94, 98, 103, 115
  Aceca 33, 40, *42*, 59, *61*, 62,
    65, 103, 157
  Acedes 33
  Autocarrier 26
  Buckland tourer 33–6, *35*,
    50, 58
  Greyhound 33, *40*, 77
  Invalid car 36–7, *36*, 40
  Le Mans coupe 7, 179
  Le Mans racer (1958) *53*, 76
  ME2500 42
  ME3000 40–2, *43*
  MkIV 7, 10, 13, 44, *44*, 45,
    79, 174, 178, *180–1*, 190
  Montlhèry Six Sports 32, *32*
  Petite 36–7, *37*
  Record breakers 31, *31*
  Sociable 26, 27, *27*
AC Cars Ltd 6, 7, 11, 26–45,
  39, 61, 66, 75, 77, 83, 90–2,
  126, 134, 143, 175–8, 190
  AC (Acedes) Ltd 32
  AC (Ecosse) 42
  AC Cars (Scotland) Ltd 42, 43
  Auto Carriers Ltd 26
  Auto Carriers (1911) Ltd 26
  Autocars and Accessories
    Ltd 26
  Brooklands works 45, 175
  Taggs Island works 37
  Thames Ditton works 6, 26,
    32, *32*, 50, 75, 97, 103
  West Norwood works 26, *28*
AC Owners Club 74

AFN Ltd 29
Alan Mann Racing 73
Aldington, brothers 29, 30
Alfin brakes 48, 54, 55, *57*
All-American Racers 196
Allard 11, 14, 17, 18, 46, 75
AMA 71
Amon, Chris 166, 178
Angliss, Brian 7, 43, 44, 45,
  137, 174–8
Arning, Klaus 115, 183, 198
Aston Martin 11, 14, 18, 19,
  22, 23, 64, 69
Aston Martin, cars
  DB2/4 46
  DB4GT 98
  DBR1/300 *24*, *25*
  DBR3 *20*
  DBR4/250 23, 24
Atkins, 'Tommy' *136*, 178
Attwood, Dickie 152
Autokraft 7, 43, *137*, 175–8
  Autokraft MkIV (*see* AC
    MkIV)
  CP (Cobra Parts) 43, 174
  CP Autokraft 43
Automobile Club of
  Argentina 17
Autosport 50, 52, 62, 103

Bailey, Ernie 37, 38, 50, 52
Bailey, Len 201
Balchowski, Max 160
Beidler, Charles 126–7
Benavides, Jim 114
Bird, Barrie 74, 179
Blakeley, David 59
BMC *20*, 69
BMW 328 29–30
Bohanna, Peter 40
Bolster, John 52, 103
Bolton, Peter 103, 143, *143*,
  147, 179
Bondurant, Bob 150, 156, 166,
  167, 168, 170, *171*
Bonneville 19, *20*
  '200mph Club' 21

Bordinat, Gene 86–7
  Bordinat Cobra 86–7
  Cougar II 87
Brabham, Jack 52
Bristol Aeroplane Co (and
  Bristol Cars) 30, 61
  Bristol 407 30, 65, 66
British Anzani 29, 30, 32
Brock, Peter 11, 25, 68, 69, 79,
  80, 130, 135, 157, 159, 160,
  161, 164, 165, 198
  Brock Racing
    Enterprises 160
Brock, Ray 15, 72
Brown, Bob 142
Brown, Charlie 17
Brown, David *18*
Brownlow Sheet Metal Co 79
Bruce, Hon Victor and Mrs 31,
  32
Brunell, Kitty 33
Brunell, W.J. 31, 33
Buckland Body Works 37, 50
Buell, Temple 23

California Metal Shaping
  Co 161
Car & Driver 160, 178
Car Life 82
Carroll Shelby
  Enterprises 202
  Carroll Shelby School of High
    Performance Driving 22,
    66, 68, 69, 80, 160
  Carroll Shelby Sports
    Cars 22, 23
Carrozzeria Grand Sport 166,
  167
Carrozzeria Touring 48
Centro Sud 23
Chaparral 22, 142
Chequered Flag *136*, *155*
Cherryhomes, Roy 17, 19
Chinetti, Luigi 22
Chrysler, cars
  Dodge CSX 202
  Dodge Polara 500 111

Dodge Viper 11, 202–8
Plymouth Sport Fury 111
Shelby Dakota pick-up 202
(*see also* Sunbeam Tiger)
Christy, John 69
Clark, Jim 52
'Cobra II' 117
Cole, Ed 66
Cole, Tommy 11
Collins, Peter 18, 19
Conner, Bob *71*
Cooper cars 46, 47, 48, 52
Cooper Monaco 142
Cosby, Bill 127
Cougar-Cobra 201
Cramer, Peyton 164
Crosley 'Copper Brazed'
    engine 77
Cross, Lord 103
Cunningham, Briggs 11, 14,
    67
Cunningham Continental 14

Davis, Cliff 38, *38*, *47*, 48, *49*,
    50, 52, 59
Davison, Vin 37, 38, 50, 51,
    52, 54, *60*, 74
Daytona coupe 6, 7, 11, 12, 69,
    103, 107, 108, 109, 135,
    143, 150, 151, 152, 154,
    156, 157–172, *158*, *169*,
    170, *171*, *172*, 179
De Tomaso, Alessandro 69,
    160, 166, 179
De Tomaso, cars
  Mangusta 160, 179, 200
  Pantera 160, 179, 200
Diablo 40–1
Don, Kaye 31
Dopudja, Mike 165
Dowd, Al 98
'Dragonsnake' 102, 139
Duncan, Dale 18

Earl, Harley 66
Ecosse Signature 42
Ecurie Ecosse 53, 143
Edgar, John 22, 23
Edge, Selwyn Francis 29, *29*,
    30, 31, 32, 33
Edwards, Stirling 98
Electric Fuel Propulsion
    Inc 183–5
Engines
  'AC 3.6' 74
  AC six-cylinder 6, 30, 33,

    34, 36, 38, 46, 54, *55*, 58, 59,
    65, 67
  BMW six-cylinder 30, *40*,
    61, *63*, 66
  Bristol six-cylinder 6, 11,
    14, 38, *38*, *39*, *40*, 46, 50, *53*,
    58, 59, 61–2, *62*, 63, *63*, 65,
    69, 75
  Cadillac V8 11
  Chevrolet V8 70
  Chrysler V8 6, 19, 30, 64, 66
  Cosworth, Ford 45
  Coventry-Climax 52
  Daimler V8 70
  Fivet 26
  Ford six-cylinder 6, 38, 46,
    58, 59, 64, 65, 70
  Ford 221cu in V8 14, 72, *73*
  Ford 260cu in V8 11, 46, 73,
    74, 79, 80–1, 95, 111
  Ford 289cu in V8 11, *97*,
    99–100, 139, *141*
  Ford 302cu in V8 175
  Ford 352cu in V8 175
  Ford 390cu in V8 109–10
  Ford 427cu in V8 6, 7, 11,
    106, 107–8, 110–11, *113*,
    125, 130–4, 175
  Ford 428cu in V8 11, 130–34
  Ford Indianapolis V8 93
  Ford V6 41
  Gurney-Weslake V8 *81*
  Jaguar 6-cylinder 70
  Jaguar V12 *177*
  Oldsmobile 425cu in V8 131
  Rover/Buick V8 70, 72, 175
Evans, Dave 11, 70, 72, 73, 75,
    79
Everly, John 137, 138
Eyston, Capt George 21

Fairey Aviation 33, 36
Fairman, Jack *18*
Fangio, Juan Manuel 22, 23
Feinstein, Sam 155
Ferrari 10, 12, 18, 70, 107,
    135, 139, 147, 152, 154,
    156, 157, 167–8
Ferrari, cars
  121LM 22
  166 Barchetta 38, *48*, 48, 50
  250GT 98–9
  250GTB 161
  250GTO 142, 150, 161, 163,
    167, 168
  275GTB 168

  250/275LM 108, 110, 119,
    154, *158*, 167, 170
  375 22
  400 Superamerica 98–9
  500 Testarossa 22
  750 Monza 21
  F40 99
  Testarossa 96
Ferrari, Enzo 10, 21, 22,
    154–5, 196
Feutel, Ed 156
FIA 7, 10, 12, 23, 82, 107, 110,
    119, 126, 138, 139, 147,
    150, 151, 152, 154, 159,
    166, 167, 170
Fiat 500 'Topolino' 47, 52
Fields, Jeanne 16
Fitch, John 67
'Flip-Top' 427 prototype 7, 110
'Flying Shingle' 109
Ford, cars
  Fairlane 14, 72, 73, *74*, *201*
  Falcon 72, 94
  Falcon Sprint 73, 80
  Galaxie 11, 72, 110, 112,
    113
  GT40 14, 70, 97, 102, 108,
    114, 115, 119, 126, 135,
    143, *158*, 160, 163, 164,
    165, 166, 167, 168, 170,
    196–7, *197*, *198*
  Lincoln Capri 71
  Mustang (including Shelby
    Mustangs) 14, 79, 102,
    109, 114, 115, 173,
    196–201, *199*
  Thunderbird 67, 87, 110
Ford, Edsel II 175
Ford, Henry II 71–2, *72*, 112
Ford Motor Co 7, 10, 11, 44,
    45, 66, 75, 77, 79, 80, *84*, 86,
    88, 97, 107, 114, 118, 134,
    158, 164, 165, 168, 170,
    175–8, 183, 196–202
Ford Advanced Vehicles 70,
    127, 165
Ford Engineering 115
Ford France 167
Ford Motor Credit 178
Ford Safety Campaign 11
Ford Special Vehicle
    Operations 175
'Total Performance' 11, 70,
    73, 102, 111, 196–7
Frazer-Nash 27, 29, *38*, 48,
    109

Frère, Paul 19
Frey, Don 75, 158, 196
Friedman, Dave 163
Frua, coachbuilders 40, *41*, 134, 179

Garrad, Ian 201
Geddes, Ray 75, 116, 197
General Motors 11, 32, 66, 67, 68, 70, 80, 108, 160, 162
General Motors, cars
  'Cadet' styling exercise 160
  Chevrolet Corvair 80, 160
  Chevrolet Corvette 66, 67, *67*, 80, 86, 98–9, 136, 142, 175, 197
  Chevrolet Corvette Grand Sport 77, 108, 110, 166
  Chevrolet Corvette Sting Ray 68, 160, 162
  Chevrolet Impala SS 111
  Chevrolet Monza 73
  Pontiac Grand Prix 111
Ghia, coachbuilders 127, 160, 179, *182*, 200
Gillett, Thomas 29, 31, *31*, 32
Giugiaro, Giorgietto 160
Gomm, Maurice 53
Gordon, Bailey 16
Grant, Allen 168, *169*, *171*
Grant, Jerry 151
Gray, Eric 50
Gregory, Masten 17, 22, 23
Grossman, Bob 67
Guichet, Jean 150
Gulf-Mirage 197
Gurney, Dan 23, 139, 142, 150, 151, 166, 167

Halibrand wheels 108, 119, *121*, 127, 130, 138, 142
Hall, Dick 22, 23
Hall, Jim 22, 23
Hamilton, Duncan 19, *20*
Hawker, Harry 31
Healey, Donald 11, 19, *20*, 21, 69
Healey, cars 67
  100S and record breakers 21
  Austin-Healey 100-4 46, 59
  Austin-Healey 3000 *69*
Henderson, Jock 183
Hertz Sports Car Club 199
Hill, Graham 52

Hill, Phil 21, 142, 150, 166, 167
Hoffman, Max 22
Holbert, Bob 142, 150, 163, 165
Holman & Moody 137
Hope, Major 52–3
Hot Rod 15, 72
Howard, Benny 162
Hudson, Skip 142, 159
Hugus, Ed 85, 86, 90, 143, 147, 157, 196
Hurlock brothers 11, 32, 37, 50, 74
  Hurlock, Charles 32, 50, 51, 65, 70, 75, 103
  Hurlock, Derek 33, 40, 41, 50, 103, 175
  Hurlock, William 32, 50
Hutton, Barbara 109

Iacocca, Lee 11, 70, *72*, 196, 197, 202, 203
Ireland, Innes 167
Iso *158*

Jackson-Moore, Roy 21
Jaguar, cars
  C-type 19
  E-type 98–9
  XK120 17, 46, 59
Jensen 11, 69, 202
Johnson, Bob 142, 150
Jones, Dan 87
Jopp, Peter 143, 147

Karsh, Herb 162
Keck, Hal 155, 156, 168
Kimberly Cup 18
Kimberly, 'Gentleman' Jim 18
King Cobra 196
Kranefuss, Mike 175
Krause, Billy 6, 85, 136, 137, 138

Lamborghini, Ferruccio 10
Lamborghini Countach 96
Lawrence, Eloise 15
Legislation 12, 173
Leicester, Harry 52
'Le Mans Replica' 142, 150
Leonard, Lionel 47, *47*, 48
Lister, Brian 48
Lola 196
Lowther, Ed 55, 156
Lutz, Bob 203

Mabee, Guy 19
Mac, Roger *155*
MacDonald, Dave 138, 139, 142, 150, 163, 165
Marczewski, Z.T. 50–1, 183
Maserati 21, 69
Maserati, cars
  250F 22
  300S 23
  450S 23
  T61 Birdcage 25, 68
McCord Radiator Co 94
McDonald, Dave 42
McLaren, Bruce 159, *169*
Miles, Ken 7, 11, 97, 98, 107, 108, *108*, 109, 110, 113, 116, 127, 138, 142, 150, 155, 157, 159, 161, 163, *169*, 198
Monte Carlo or Bust (film) 174
Monte Carlo Rally 31, *32*, 33, 73
Moon, Dean 25, 74, 79
Morton, John 107
Moss, Stirling 23, *25*, 103, 146, 150
Motor 58
Munaron, Gino 22
Muther, Rick *170*

Napier, Lt-Col John S. 29
NASCAR 70–2, *71*, 112, 117, 130–1
Neerspach, Jochen 151, 166, 167
Negstadt, Bob 115, 116, 183

Ogier, John 52
Olsen, John 159, 161, 163

Pabst, Augie 137
Paramount Pictures 7, 174, 189
Paravano, Tony 21, 22
Parsons, John 42
Paxton-supercharged 427s 127
Petersen, Walt 70
Piper, David 156
'Pooper' 109
Porsche, cars
  550 Spyder 22
  959 99 162
  Turbo 96
Portwine, John 26, 29, 31, 32, 33

RAC Rally   33, 58
Races and circuits
  Aintree   *20*
  Bridgehampton   142, 155,
    167, 168
  Brands Hatch   *39*, *151*, 156
  Brooklands   31
  Carrera Panamericana   21,
    71
  Castle Rock   25
  Coppa di Enna   171
  Cuban GP   22
  Daytona   11, 139, 150, 156,
    163, 168
  Goodwood   23, *25*, 48, *49*, 62,
    154, 167
  Grants Despair   22
  Indianapolis   23, 196
  Italian GP   23
  Le Mans   6, 7, 11, 14, *18*, 23,
    24, 48, *48*, 64, *67*, 70, 87,
    103, 143–50, *143*, *146*, 152,
    157, 162, 164, 166–7, 168,
    170, 196
  *Mil Kilometres de la Ciudad
    de Buenos Aires*   17
  Montlhèry   31, *31*
  Monza   154, 167, 168, *171*
  Mount Washington   22
  Nassau Speed Weeks   7, 22,
    110, 137
  Nurburgring   23, 151–2,
    166, 168
  Oulton Park   22
  Palm Springs   22
  Pebble Beach   22
  Pikes Peak Hillclimb   70, 72
  Reims   167, 170
  Riverside   6, 7, 22, 23, 25,
    68, 79, 85, 103, 108, 109,
    135, 136, 138, 163
  Seattle Seafair Races   22
  Sebring   7, 18, 22, 23, 107,
    142, 150, 156, 163, 165,
    168, 170, *170*
  Silverstone   19, *24*, *60*, *64*,
    77, 116
  Spa   23, 151, 166, 168
  Supercortemaggiore GP   19
  Syracuse GP   22
  Targa Florio   22, 151, 166
  Tour de France   154, 164,
    167
  Tourist Trophy   22, 23, 154,
    154, 167

Radford, Harold   164–5
Railton   14
Raymond Mays cylinder heads
    65
Remington, Phil   11, 97, 98,
    103, 116, 138, 159, 198
Replicas   13
  Dax   53, *176–7*
  DJ Sportscars   53
  SAAC definition   189–90
Reventlow, Lance   25, 97, 109
'Riverside Replica'   138
Road & Track   82, 127, 174
Rootes Group   201–2
Rudd, Ken   62, 63, 64, 65, 70
Ruddspeed   65

Saint-Auban, Bernard   167
Salvadori, Roy   19, 22, 23, 52,
    178
Sanderson, Ninian   103, 143,
    143, 147
Scarab   25, 97, 109
SCCA   17, 23, 64, 69, 82, 107,
    118, 119, 126, 135, 136,
    139, 142, 150, 155, 160,
    197–8, 199
Scheberies, Jerry   70
Schlesser, Jo   150, 152, 168,
    169, 170
Sears, Chris   48
Sears, Jack   *151*, *154*, 170, *172*,
    179
Selby, T.V.   33
'Semi/Competition'   *112*, *120*,
    124, 126–30, 134, *152*, 178,
    181
Settember, Tony   156
Shelby American
Shelby American Automobile
    Club   79, 138, 160, 189
  Shelby Automotive   200
  Shelby Parts &
    Accessories   200
  Shelby Racing   200
*Shelby American World
    Registry*   79, 187
Shelby, Anne   15
Shelby Can-Am racer   160
Shelby, Carroll   *passim*
Shelby, Warren Hall   15–16
Shelby Mustang (*see* Ford, cars)
Shelby's Wildlife   14
Sidney, Harry   70
Spencer, Lew   150

Sports Car Graphic   69, 80–2
Sports Car International   162
Sports Illustrated, Driver of the
    Year   22
Stables, Robin   40
Stirrat, Robert F.   72
Sunbeam Tiger   109, *200*,
    201–2
Sunburst wheels   *126*, *128*, 130
Sunday Times, The   *146*, 150
'Super Coupe' 427   7, 134, 135,
    160, 164–5
Sutherland, Craig   165
Suttcliffe, Peter   168

Tasca Ford   90
Terlingua Boys Ranch   202
Terlingua Racing Team   202
Terry, Len   201
Thompson, Dick   170, *172*
Threlfall, Chris   48
Timanus, John   25, 160, *170*
Tojeiro, John   11, 37, 41, 46,
    50, 52–3, 58, 76, 183
Tojeiro chassis   6, 37, 38, *38*,
    46, 47, *47*, 48, *49*, 50, 51,
    52–3, *53*, 54, 58, 76
Traco   98
Trintignant, Maurice   167
Triumph TR2   46
'The Turd'   110
Turner, Alan   74, 103, 116,
    179, 183
Turner, Jack   64

USRRC   25, 107, 135, 138, 139,
    142, 143, 150, 155

Vauxhall Motors   32

Weller, John   26, 27, 29, 30,
    31, 32, 33
Whiteaway, Ted   64
Whitehead, Graham   19
Whitmore, Sir John   168
Wilkins, Ed   17
Wilkinson, Wilkie   53
Willment, John   103, *151*
Willment racing coupe   127
Wing, Roger   70
Winterbottom, Eric   52
Woods, Aubrey   42
Woolfe, John   124, *137*
Wyer, John   18, 19, *19*, 165,
    170, 196, 197
Wyss, Wallace A.   14